STANDING UP
STANDING BACK

STANDING UP
STANDING BACK

BOB TAYLOR
with
Patrick Murphy

WILLOW BOOKS
Collins
8 Grafton Street, London W1
1985

To the two main guiding influences in
my life: my wife Cathy, and John Ikin –
coach, advisor and friend who died in
the week of my retirement

Willow Books
William Collins Sons & Co Ltd
London · Glasgow · Sydney · Auckland
Toronto · Johannesburg

First published 1985
© Bob Taylor

British Library Cataloguing in Publication Data

Taylor, Bob
Standing up, standing back.
1. Taylor, Bob   2. Cricket players—
Great Britain—Biography
I. Title   II. Murphy, Pat
796.35'8'0924   GV915.T/

ISBN 0 00 218114 2

Set in Times New Roman
by Ace Filmsetting Ltd, Frome, Somerset
Printed and bound in Great Britain by
William Collins Sons & Co Ltd, Glasgow

CONTENTS

CHAPTER 1

FROM BLACK PLIMSOLLS TO SPIKES

At just nine years of age, I was determined to be a wicketkeeper. Such considerations as playing for my country or even getting paid to stand behind the stumps formed no part of my childlike ambitions, but no one was going to stop me from wearing the gloves. The simple reason for that was my ego. Now this may surprise some who kindly remark on my self-effacing qualities, but I have always been quietly confident of my abilities and obsessively determined to do the very best I could with them. Even at the age of nine. I can remember the very day when I decided I wanted more from the game of cricket than just being a bystander while the bigger lads starred. There I was, standing on the boundary edge during a game at Stoke St Peter's Primary School and I thought to myself, 'This is boring, I want to get involved.' I asked my sports master if I could have a go behind the stumps and, from that day on, I was hooked.

My ego had been fuelled during the school football season. I fancied myself as a pretty nifty centre-forward (even though I was as short as a fag-end!) and the fact that I regularly popped a few goals in convinced me. Every Monday morning, our sports master would put up a report of Saturday's game on the school notice-board, underlining the scorers in red ink. I craved to see my name in red ink and the same applied when I started to keep wicket. 'Stumped Taylor' or 'caught Taylor' meant a lot to me: I knew that cricket was a team game, and I hope I have never forgotten that fact, but I needed to be involved, to be good at the sport. Personal success was important and I was mentally tough while still in short trousers. It was important to play something more than a mere bit-part in any team game.

Sport was always a vital part of my childhood and I was encouraged by a loving, close-knit family. My two sisters may have despaired of my obsession with sport, but they never told me so.

My father actively encouraged me – he had played professional football for Sunderland, but had lost an eye in the war, so he channelled his energies into supporting my juvenile fantasies. We lived just around the back of Stoke City Football Club and most nights I would be found playing cricket, tennis or football under the gas lights. Like most backstreet kids, we painted three stumps on a wall or relied on a dustbin for the stumps. No one challenged me when I announced I was to be permanent wicket-keeper and I loved it. When the ball was sent down the leg side I would scuttle across behind the dustbin and gather it – even then a leg side 'take' meant a lot to me! I suppose I was lucky with my physique – small, and light on my feet – but it all seemed very natural to me. Infinitely better than standing at third man, waiting for an edge!

There must have been something of merit in my displays behind the stumps because my sports master, Stan Brassington, proceeded to introduce me to a world that was fabulously exciting to a naive boy like me. At the age of 13 I was taken to Bignall End Cricket Club, 15 miles away from my home. It was the first time I had been in a motor car – that was adventure enough for me – and when I got there I was captivated by the atmosphere. A miner's welfare club dominated the scene, with a large pavilion attached. There were also snooker and committee rooms and overall a sense of tradition and care. In the cricket pavilion, there were wooden benches around the walls, and a wooden floor that gave you splinters in your bare feet. Pads and bats were kept in lockers and they were lovingly nurtured by an unselfish, kind man named Aaron Lockett. He was nearly 60 at the time and had been a fine allrounder in the Lancashire League. Aaron had returned to his home town and proceeded to save the club a lot of money by sewing the old pads and gloves, and keeping everything neat and tidy in the pavilion. I can see him now – white haired, glasses on the end of his nose, for all the world like a cobbler – attending to the unsung duties of keeping a club going. The smell of linseed oil and rubber handles of bats comes back to me as I think of the tremendously happy times I enjoyed at Bignall End.

Aaron was to be my guide and mentor in my early days at the club – and, Lord knows, I needed some help. I played my first match at the age of 13 in the Kidsgrove League Under-18 section, and my education was about to begin. In common with others at the time, I had no proper cricket gear: I managed a white shirt, but had to make do with black plimsolls, grey flannels and pads that went halfway up my chest. On my way out to keep wicket for my club for the first time, I was asked if I was wearing a box. 'What's a box?' I asked, in all innocence, and was surprised to hear everyone laughing themselves hoarse. I soon found out how useful an abdominal protector could be!

My love affair with cricket was now well and truly consummated. What a thrill it was to play with older cricketers in such superb conditions! I wanted to get up to Bignall End every night, despite the need to take two buses: Mr Brassington would give me tea at his house after school and then it would be off to the club to learn more about the game. Money was tight in the Potteries in those days and I often wonder where my parents found the cash to pay my travelling expenses and get me some decent kit – but they did, and I hope I showed my gratitude often enough.

Stan Brassington also helped broaden my horizons by giving me a tantalising glimpse of Test cricket. He took me to Old Trafford to see the 1955 South Africans, then a year later against the Australians I saw part of Laker's Match. I am disappointed to say that I missed that dramatic last day when Jim Laker finished up with 19 wickets in the match, but I saw enough earlier in the game to whet my appetite. I plucked up enough courage to ask for one or two autographs during both games and, a few years later, fate dealt a double twist. One of the autographs was that of Jackie McGlew who captained the South Africans on my first-class debut in 1960 – and another was that of Jim Laker, who later played for Norton against me in the North Staffs League!

That was my sum total of watching first-class cricket until I joined Derbyshire, but I was lucky that another mentor was at hand to give me valuable insights into the professional game. John Ikin had played 18 times for England while with Lancashire, but he was born and bred a Bignall End lad. When his first-class career ended, he returned home. To my eternal good fortune, that coincided with the arrival at the club of a little shrimp called R. W. Taylor. He obviously saw something of promise in my displays, and John Ikin never stopped encouraging and guiding me. He had so much to offer a greenhorn like me; I just drank in his knowledge and never tired of listening to his anecdotes and tips. It seemed almost preordained that my captain would be John Ikin when I first played for Staffordshire and also when I made my debut in first-class cricket for Minor Counties – and so it proved. Could any youngster of ambition have been luckier?

Thanks to John Ikin and Aaron Lockett, I made progress at Bignall End. I first played in the league at 15 (mum had bought me some white flannels by then – and a box!) and cricket simply became a constant delight. I cannot remember how good I was, compared with other keepers of my age, but one day I saw the man I wanted to copy. At that time, Keith Andrew was keeping wicket for Northamptonshire and John Ikin told me what a superb technician he was. He had played just once for England, despite his brilliance. It seemed that the England selectors preferred the more flamboyant qualities and the superior batting of Godfrey Evans to the quiet excellence of Keith Andrew. One day, I managed to witness his skills at first hand, when Northants came to Burslem (one of the Five Towns) to play a benefit match. He made it look so easy – standing up to the spinning wiles of George Tribe and Jack Manning and anticipating the thunderbolts from Frank Tyson when he stood back. From that day on, I modelled myself on Keith Andrew; I wanted to have that quiet air of confidence, that unhurried quality. Looking back on it now, I suppose that ambition stemmed from the area in which I lived – unpretentious, hardworking and unspectacular – and the sort of person I am. Although I had this ego of inner steel, I did not parade it, preferring to keep my eyes and ears open and deferring to my elders and betters.

Of course, I did not dare approach Keith Andrew for advice – indeed he was still 'Mr Andrew' to me long after I had started in county cricket. I just followed his career with the devotion of a disciple and felt for him when he was brought back by England for just one game in 1963. He conceded only three byes in a West Indies total of 501, he stood up to Ted Dexter's erratic, medium-pace swingers and then he made a brave nightwatchman's 15 against Hall, Griffith, Sobers and Gibbs. His reward was to be dropped for the next Test, to be replaced by a superior batsman in Jim Parks. It seemed that the batting of a wicketkeeper was more important than his abilities on the other side of the stumps. Little did I realise that the ill fortune of my hero would later be emulated several times by myself at the hands of the England selectors!

By the time I was 15 there were no doubts in my mind: I wanted to play county cricket. I wanted to be a poorer version of

Keith Andrew. Everyone was so kind and supportive to me at Bignall End that I felt I owed it to myself and to the club to do the best I could. Grim reality was just around the corner to put an end to those youthful fantasies, and the man responsible was my biggest supporter. John Ikin was asked by me to see if I could join the Lancashire groundstaff, but he said that was impossible. Mr Ikin said counties would not take on young players until they had done their national service first (yes, I am that old!), and that the best thing for me to do in the meantime was to learn a trade to get some security. I know his advice was correct and sincere, but I felt terribly disillusioned. How could I possibly wait six years? That was a very long time when you had no idea just how good you were. At least Mr Ikin's fatherly advice awakened me to the need to think about something other than cricket and I managed to land an apprenticeship as a signwriter with the Midlands Electricity Board at Stoke. The MEB were very good to me during my stint with them – I was given time off to play for Staffordshire in the summer while enjoying full-time work in the winter. In those days, an apprenticeship was the goal for a working-class lad like me and the things I learned have stood me in good stead when I occasionally pick up the paint brush or do some home decorating!

At least I now had some security, much to the relief of my family – but my cricketing ambitions were not quashed. I played my first game for Staffordshire at Norton when I was 16, despite the valiant efforts of the gateman to keep me out. I was so excited at the prospect of playing on the same ground where Sir Frank Worrell had been a professional that I got there far too early on the first morning. The gateman took one look at this tiny figure clutching a green bag and said, 'The boys' entrance is round the corner.' I squeaked, 'But I'm playing.' Of course, he would not believe me. Had I got up at the crack of dawn and changed buses three times for this? Luckily, Fred Bailey, our opening batsman, came along just as I was getting desperate and vouched for me. That Staffordshire team contained three England players of the past and future – John Ikin, David Steele and myself. David and I have known each other since 1957 and he ended up captaining me for a season at Derbyshire. I am two months older and our families lived ten miles away, so we soon struck up a close friendship which still exists today, despite David's reluctance to buy me a drink whenever it's his turn! At the age of just 16 we discovered we had something particularly personal in common. We were getting changed for practice and he said, 'I can see a grey hair on you, Robert,' and I replied, 'You're not doing so bad yourself, Steeley.' Since then, we have monitored the march of progress of grey hairs on our head and I must say the white-haired old gentleman from Brown Edge wins hands down!

Those four summers spent playing for Staffordshire were happy ones. Mr Ikin was the captain and I lacked nothing in the way of advice and guidance from him. Somehow I managed to give a good account of myself behind the stumps without worrying unduly. I seemed to have worked out the basics early on – the next ball was the important one, not the previous delivery that I had fumbled. The ability to concentrate appeared to come easily to me, perhaps because it was a sheer delight to keep wicket to good bowlers. My footwork was satisfactory – as you would expect from a teenager who took ballroom dancing lessons at the Sid Perkins and Edna Duffield School of Dancing at Newcastle-under-Lyme! I could get round the dance floor neatly enough and David Steele and I cut quite a dash at the Palais on a Saturday night when we discovered the fair sex!

Life was good and I could not ask for anything more from anyone. Money was tight, but we were used to that: the Potteries had long been an area where unemployment is a threat and at least our family were all in jobs. My employers were very understanding and I was taking steps to get some security by learning a trade. Yet the thought of county cricket still gnawed away at me; I was coming into contact with several first-class cricketers through charity games and the occasional Staffordshire fixtures only whetted my appetite for the real thing. The county scores in the paper were avidly devoured by me and I listened to the Test match radio broadcasts whenever possible. Finally, in 1960, a double breakthrough. I made my first-class debut and Derbyshire asked me to play some Second XI cricket.

It was just my luck that Mr Ikin was on hand to conquer my nerves as I walked out at Stoke with the Minor Counties side to play the South Africans. He was captaining a good team – Phil Sharpe and Jack Birkenshaw were also included – but we were no match for a strong opposition that included the likes of Jackie McGlew, John Waite, Hughie Tayfield, Athol McKinnon and Neil Adcock. Now Adcock was easily the fastest bowler I had faced and he dismissed me for nought, caught at leg slip by Sid O'Linn – the first of many noughts, I fear. In the second innings, I had the mortification of facing an over of slow full tosses down the leg side by Jackie McGlew, the man who had given me his autograph five years earlier. I missed most of the slow offerings and he got me lbw for 11. More importantly, I let through just four byes in their total of 373, standing up to the spin of Jack Birkenshaw and John Ikin for long periods. It seemed to go reasonably well for me and Derbyshire played me four times in their Second XI afterwards. One of those games nearly gave me heart failure. The Derbyshire coach, Denis Smith, had arranged to pick me up at Leek to take me to St Helens for the match against Lancashire. I got there ridiculously early (of course) and waited. Still I waited. An hour after the agreed time, I was convinced that Mr Smith had decided I was not good enough and that he had found someone else at short notice to keep wicket, leaving me to kick my heels in Leek. Just as I was about to make my crestfallen way home, he drove up and we were on our way. I was too timorous to ask where he had been, but I often wonder what would have happened to R. W. Taylor's cricket career if I had not shown some patience that day.

The Derbyshire connection came from another stroke of luck. Cliff Gladwin had just left the county after a long and honourable career as a fast bowler. He joined Longton in the North Staffordshire League and it seems he tipped off his old county after he played at Bignall End. Unknown to me, Mr Smith came to watch me and must have reported favourably. I shall never forget the day that my life changed: it was a drab, rainy afternoon at the Goodyear Sports Ground in Wolverhampton. Staffordshire were playing Durham and we were off the field for rain when I was told, 'There are two gentlemen here to see you from Derbyshire County Cricket Club.' I was reading a magazine at the time and I threw it to the floor and was on my feet in a flash. The club chairman, Mr Robin Buckston, and a former Secretary, Mr Will Taylor, asked me to have a private chat with them in their car and, with a beating heart, I readily agreed. The conversation was unreal: 'Have you ever considered a career in county cricket, Robert?' I thought to myself, 'For the last ten years,' but murmured something suitably modest. 'Have you got a car, Robert?' they asked. 'Oh no, sir,' I replied. 'Well you soon will have,' I was told. I thought, 'How amazing – they're going to pay me as well!' The sum of £350 a year was mentioned, but for all I cared they could have made it 350 pence. All I wanted to see was the dotted line where I could sign my name.

I had promised myself I would sign, but I felt I owed it to my family and the MEB to discuss the situation. We had a big family pow-wow on the matter, during which I managed to convince everyone I knew what I was doing, that I had an inner conviction that I could make the grade, that I would be forever restless if I spurned a golden opportunity. My apprenticeship was a worry – in those days lads of my humble background did not break their indentures with one year to go unless there was an overwhelmingly important reason. Cricket must have seemed a flimsy reason to some people, but the MEB were very good about it. Indeed they allowed me to come back and work for them in the next two winters as I made my way with Derbyshire.

Fundamentally I wanted to achieve something with my life. Before I was out of primary school I had this strong streak of self-motivation: nothing was handed to you on a plate, you had to work very hard to make the best of everything. I sensed that I had a talent to keep wicket, that in every other way I was just a normal kid with narrow horizons from a protective, working-class community. I still wanted to be part of that community – to this day, I am a proud son of the Potteries – and the fact that Derby was so near to my home was very encouraging. There was no danger of feeling homesick, the bus service would see to that. Above all, I sensed that the gods were on my side. John Ikin had guided me as captain for Bignall End, Staffordshire and Minor Counties: how many youngsters of my background were getting such caring tuition from such an eminent man? My sports master, Stan Brassington, and my first mentor, Aaron Lockett, had been there at just the right time. So was Cliff Gladwin, when he came to play at Bignall End and happened to notice me. I could never claim that I was unlucky, that I was stuck away in a cricketing backwater. Without realising it at the time, the scouting network was very advanced in Staffordshire, because we were not a championship county. As a result, every neighbouring county kept tabs on potential talent. Things could hardly have gone better for me as my great adventure started.

CHAPTER 2

EARLY DAYS WITH DERBYSHIRE

One April evening in 1961, I found myself walking towards Stoke train station with a feeling of exhilaration. I was about to start my county cricket career the next day, when I was due to report to the ground at Derby for pre-season training. I was accompanied on the walk by my father and Cathy Hood, the girl I was to marry 18 months later. We had met at the local Palais in Stoke and, although she knew nothing about cricket, she soon realised the fire that burned within me. That April night stays in my memory: my father carried my suitcase while I chattered away to Cathy about my ambitions. I was getting paid to play the game I loved, I was going to learn so much. England caps were, of course, beyond my imagination; I was content with the three-year contract I had signed. Apparently the club had to give me such a long contract because I was from a non-championship county. I certainly wasn't complaining – it gave me that much longer to prove myself. With my twentieth birthday three months away, I was to live away from home for the first time in my life.

Not even the poor facilities at the county ground could dampen my excitement. I knew nothing of cricketing luxuries and I was far too thrilled to bother about the paint peeling off the dressing-room walls, the bird droppings that invariably tumbled through the ceiling of the indoor nets, the showers that fitfully functioned and the toilet in our dressing-room that gave off such an appalling odour. It was to be many years – following several England tours – before I became embarrassed at the set-up at Derby, and the splendid modernisations of the 1980s were not before time. Yet all that was in the future: playing county cricket was all that mattered. In any event, I had already experienced a strong dose of reality two months earlier, in February 1961. My father and I came over from Stoke to formalise my signing and when we got off the bus we automatically walked over to the grandstand, where we assumed the club offices were situated. Not so – the Ministry of Agriculture owned that building, so we were directed around the corner to a poky little office, where we found the secretary. It did not matter: my cricket education was far more important than plush surroundings; after all, life in the Potteries is far from fancy!

Pre-season training in those days would be an absolute joke to the modern county pro. In the first week it consisted of a couple of laps of running, then home at lunchtime. Over the next fortnight we would have some running either side of lunch. If the weather was bad, there would be a spot of indoor nets. Sam Weaver, the Derby County footballer, was our physio at the time and he didn't believe in exerting us unduly – a spot of stretching, and some gentle jogging was all he prescribed for the rigours that lay ahead. At the time, I was a semi-professional footballer with Port Vale, so I had no trouble with these superficial exercises. How different in the last decade! Despite my advancing years, I have been expected to keep up with the youngsters during pre-season training that resembles a commando course. I often thought of those senior players of the early 1960s and how they would enjoy all those shuttle sprints, cross-country runs and press-ups that are practised by the modern cricketer!

Despite such superficialities, there were many things I learned early on at Derby that stood me in good stead. For a start, a young player spoke only when he was asked; he was expected to listen and take in the cricketing knowledge that was being passed around. I called the senior players 'Mr', and all of the juniors had to knock on the dressing-room door before entering. In those days, we still had the distinction between amateurs and professionals, but as we only had two regular amateurs – Donald Carr and Bill Richardson – the senior pros were treated with great respect. That was only right – they had done the hard work to get playing respectability, so it was logical that they deserved their status. I was amazed at how knowledgeable the senior pros were. At the start of every season, Charlie Lee, Les Jackson, Derek Morgan and a few others would sit down, look at the fixture list and make their forecasts. 'Now let's see, we'll beat Notts twice, and Glamorgan and Leicestershire', was the kind of thing I got used to hearing and they were invariably correct. In retrospect, that only underlines the imbalance between many county sides in those days – their forecasts of Derbyshire defeats were also inspired – but there was no doubt in my mind that they knew their profession inside out. For the first three seasons, I was fortunate enough to travel around to games with Les Jackson, Derek Morgan and Laurie Johnson, and I was very impressed at the technical knowledge of cricket they possessed. When subsequent England captains have kindly remarked on my apparent mastery of cricket's tactical intricacies, I can only point to those formative years at Derby where I learned so much.

Discipline was predictably severe in those days. Once, the senior coach, Denis Smith caught me watching a game without a jacket. I had just finished my practice with the Second XI and wanted to watch Colin Cowdrey batting for Kent against the seniors. I settled down, content that my education would be enriched by a glimpse of a master batsman, when the coach roared at me, 'Put your jacket on! Never forget who you are representing!' The fact that I was wearing cavalry twill trousers, a waistcoat and a collar and tie on a blazing hot day was irrelevant – the jacket had to be worn. Just my luck that I had brought a heavy sports jacket with me that morning! The First XI captain, Donald Carr, could be equally severe: I remember the rollickings I used to get when my lobs back to the bowler fell short and he had to bend. Mr Carr would tell me in no uncertain terms where I had let him down, and that the bowler should be able to conserve his energies between deliveries and avoid leaping around like a goalkeeper. He was absolutely right and, for the next 20 years, I tried to make things easier for the bowler in that respect.

It was a hard school, but it was the right way to bring on the youngsters. It costs nothing to be polite to one's elders, to work hard at one's chosen profession and to respect its traditions. When I hear moans from the younger breed of county professional – and the occasional Test player – I wonder how they would have shaped up two decades earlier. All the counties operated along similar lines and, even though the quality of cricket may have been less exciting than its modern counterpart, the disciplines and standards of behaviour were far superior.

Cricket wasn't the only matter I studied during my first few years at Derby. I came to grips with religion. When Cathy and I decided to marry, I agreed to convert to the Roman Catholic faith so we could share the same religious beliefs and bring up our children in unity. Because of the superficial pre-season training, I had a lot of time on my hands, so I visited the local priest several times a week and enjoyed our chats. He helped me take a more philosophical view of the world and to build on the principles I thought were important. There have been times in my career when religion has been a very important support to me.

In the early part of that 1961 season, I had no idea how near I was to a regular place in county cricket. My learning process had only just begun and I thought that the regular number one keeper, George Dawkes, was good for a few more years before I even began to press him for a place. He was 41 at the time – capped by Leicestershire as long ago as 1938 – but he seemed fit enough. He and his predecessor, Harry Elliott, had been keeping for Derbyshire for almost every season since 1920 and a young whippersnapper from Stoke was unlikely to break that monopoly in the near future, if at all. Yet the good fortune that has favoured my life was soon to help me. After beginning the 1961 season in his usual professional fashion, George Dawkes injured a knee and had to pull out of the Sussex match. That ended a run of 289 consecutive championship matches that stretched back to 1950 and ushered R. W. Taylor onto the county scene. I remember vividly the day when I heard I was in – the Club and Ground side were playing at Repton School on a baking hot afternoon. Les Jackson, our England fast bowler, was having a try-out after injury and he was getting pasted around the park by a talented young batsman by the name of Richard Hutton. Little did I realise that a decade later Richard and I would tour Australia together with a Rest of the World side! Anyway, my captain that day, Major Douglas Carr, said to me at the tea interval, 'Robert, you will be playing for the first team at home tomorrow against Sussex. George Dawkes has been injured.' I could only murmur, 'Yes, Major, thank you, Major' and tottered away, letting it sink in. Eventually I thought of Gerry Wyatt, the previous understudy to George Dawkes. Poor Gerry only ever played against the two university sides and managed under 20 games over the previous decade. He had left the staff in 1960 when I was taken on and now here was I in a county game just a month after the start of my first season. Life can be cruel sometimes.

On Wednesday, 7 June 1961 I made my championship debut and walked straight into a tense atmosphere. For some reason our fast bowler Harold Rhodes and the Sussex seamer Ian Thomson had never got on very well – all this was before my time, but I soon had first-hand knowledge of the antipathy between them. It surfaced on the last day, as we desperately blocked it out for a draw with nine wickets down. The last man to come to the wicket was Harold Rhodes – in brown suede shoes! Harold had been hit on the toe earlier in the game and he was in agony as he took guard, anxiously looking at the hole in his shoe that had been slit open to ease the bruise. Ian Thomson spotted it and, with a gleam in his eye, proceeded to bowl big inswingers aimed at Harold's injury. The air was rich between them, while at the other end the nervous debutant was ducking and weaving, trying to avoid bouncers from Don Bates. Somehow we survived the last 15 minutes of extra time, although the last ball of the match from Bates beat me all ends up and shaved the off stump.

The sequel came in the return game at Hove, when Thomson and Rhodes were at it again. Rhodes bounced Thomson, who then signalled to the dressing-room. Out came Kenny Suttle with a crash helmet and Thomson tried to put it on, in protest at the bouncers. That annoyed Arthur Fagg, the umpire, who told them to get on with the game or else they would be reported to Lord's. The Thomson/Rhodes personality clash was a rarity in those days, but don't let any old players ever tell you that it was always sweetness and light on the cricket field!

More importantly, I felt I acquitted myself well enough in that first game. I missed nothing, although my first dismissal was a little slipshod: Les Lenham nicked Derek Morgan, it hit me on the chest (I was standing up) and I had to dive forward to take it before it hit the ground. (They all count!) My county batting career began prophetically though – out first ball to a Bates bouncer that I 'gloved' to Ken Suttle at short leg. I never did get the wrists over that kind of delivery – as Messrs Lawson, Lillee, Hogg and others will readily confirm! At least I had not failed behind the stumps, and I resigned myself to a long stint in the Second XI on Dawkes' return. It was not to be: he never played again for the first team due to that troublesome knee. He retired the following year. Suddenly I was the number one keeper and all my long-held ambitions were tumbling over themselves to be realised.

I was lucky that my early days coincided with the retirement of George Dawkes and even luckier that we had a good bowling side at Derbyshire. That has been the norm until the last few years at Derby and if it has meant much anguish for our supporters that our batting has been inferior, it has done no harm at all to my wicketkeeping. Traditionally the wickets in Derbyshire favoured the bowlers and certainly I was lucky early on to keep to men of the calibre of Les Jackson, Harold Rhodes, Brian Jackson, Ian Buxton and Derek Morgan. Edwin Smith provided the only regular bout of spin with his off-breaks, but that did not stop me from standing up to some of the seamers. Initially, Buxton and Morgan wanted me to stand back to them, which was understandable because I was an unproven talent, but I made no secret that I felt I could stand up to Buxton's inswing and Morgan's off-cutters. Such confidence had been boosted during my time with the Staffordshire side, when I frequently stood up to the medium-pacers. It has always been my belief that the true test of a wicketkeeper comes when he is breathing down a batsman's neck and he has to cope with deliveries that are obscured for a split second by the batsman's pads. Off-cutters, inswingers and off-breaks are the really testing deliveries and I did not consider myself a worthy county wicketkeeper until I had proved myself in that direction.

Derbyshire's bowling strength in the 1960s meant that I would get plenty of opportunity to share in dismissals. Sure enough, I was soon earning some headlines – ten victims in the match at Chesterfield against Hampshire in 1963, my second full season. There was nothing special about any of the dismissals – all of them caught – and in vain did I tell the press boys that I just kept taking the snicks. I meant it but I was secretly pleased with my first real piece of press exposure. Cathy had started to keep a scrapbook of press cuttings and I was only too pleased to hoard any newspaper mentions for her attention. In three of the four seasons from 1962 to 1965 I took 80 or more victims – a tribute to the bowlers and the favourable wickets in the north, but also a reasonable reflection of my abilities. When my team-mates and some of the opposition started to give me regular praise, I was quietly proud. Everyone likes praise from their fellow-professionals and from the press, and I am no exception. When Fred Trueman wrote in a Sunday newspaper in 1961 that R. W. Taylor was 'another chap to keep your eye on' I was chuffed when I saw Cathy sticking the press-cutting into the scrapbook. What pleased me even more was that my seasonal tally of dismissals could have been larger in a more successful side: we lost many games by an innings, which meant that I had less opportunities than other county keepers to boost my tally. Whatever the collective form of the team, it was very important to me to do well as a wicketkeeper. The more catches and stumpings I got, the better it was for the side. It was also nice to see my name in the papers, to be in the *Daily Telegraph* averages every Wednesday and Saturday morning – back to the school notice-board again, and the name 'Taylor' underlined in red ink. To be a professional sportsman you must have pride in your perform-ance and that has always been the case with me. I reckon to be my sternest critic, I knew when my efforts had fallen below par, but I needed nobody to tell me to keep going, to strive to improve. We Potteries lads don't blow our trumpets like Yorkshiremen when we do well, but we do have a steely, inner core of resolution that makes us want to shine. I desperately wished for Derbyshire to improve as a side but a strong self-motivation meant that I would not suffer as a wicketkeeper if they didn't.

I was pleased with my progress throughout the 1960s and delighted that more and more influential people had begun to say nice things about me. Yet on two occasions I was worried about my future with the club. In 1964, I twisted my ankle playing football, but told the club I did it when I slipped on an escalator while shopping with Cathy. I figured the club would not be too happy if they knew the circumstances and my little white lie was punished by some sleepless nights as I missed the first seven games of the season. Laurie Johnson, who kept wicket occasion-ally, deputised for me and did well, standing back to everyone but Edwin Smith. As Laurie was one of our best batsmen the club seemed perfectly happy for this arrangement to continue and I began to get worried. Luckily some of the local press boys wrote a few articles attacking the decision to keep a specialist keeper out of the side and I got my place back. Who said the press were always looking for the sensational? Not me! That period might have destroyed me without their help. I had faith in my own ability but I had the feeling that the captain, Charlie Lee, valued the runs of Laurie and that my absence gave him the chance to play another batsman. My reinstatement came not a day too soon for my own peace of mind.

The other occasion came three years later, when a serious eye injury put me out for seven games. I suffered a detached retina after getting a top edge to a sweep shot against Jackie Birken-shaw's bowling on a pig of a wicket at Grace Road, Leicester. Bob Stephenson made his debut in my absence, scored 64 in his first game and impressed many good judges. I missed the last month of the 1967 season and sensed I would be under pressure in the following season. Bob and I had a very good relationship and he talked to me frankly about the need for security and whether he had a chance of displacing me full-time. I was equally frank with him and said I would be going all out to regain my place in 1968. Things worked out my way, I played in every championship match and Bob moved on to Hampshire the following year, where he was to win a championship medal and receive a good benefit. Competing against a genuine keeper had been a new experience for me since George Dawkes' retirement – Derbyshire had not bothered with an authentic number two until Bob Stephenson came along – so I had to look to my laurels when facing stern competition. It did me good and banished any illusions I might have nourished that I was indispensable.

My batting was invariably the bugbear in that first decade in county cricket. Successive captains told me I should get more runs instead of being just a useful tail-ender. I was still averaging about 14 after ten years with Derbyshire and my concentration kept letting me down. Instead of the nudging and blocking style that served me well in later years, I was too impatient and tried to play shots early in my innings. Complete concentration only came to me when I was keeping wicket – I saw myself as a specialist – yet because we were short of class batsmen in the 1960s it is true that Derbyshire needed runs from everyone. In a sense I was lucky to start when I did – before the demands of limited–overs cricket in three competitions meant that everyone had to bat at least competently and preferably at speed. When I came in to county cricket most of the wicketkeepers were specialists, with batting considered a bonus. It took me some time to get used to the particular demands of batting, and I was a sucker for the likes of Fred Trueman. 'Can you hook, son?' he bellowed at me one day, to which I replied, 'Of course.' Instead of the expected bouncer, my stumps were shattered by a fast yorker!

Despite my numerous disappointments with the bat, I was very happy at Derbyshire as the decade drew to a close. Already I had exceeded my wildest dreams by playing so many seasons. People often asked me why I stayed with Derbyshire, why I didn't join a more fashionable county. There was never any prospect of that; the club had been good enough to give me my chance and I would always be loyal to them as long as my cricket did not suffer. Money was never a problem for me, because I knew the county could not afford to pay me much more, due to a small membership and poor gates. I happily signed on every season and resolved that cash considerations would never obscure my real reasons for playing first-class cricket: I loved the game, the camaraderie among the players and the pleasure of playing a sport in the fresh air. Derbyshire may not have been all that attractive a team but we were a very happy side; we would make light of the drab facilities at the county ground, and make our own fun on tour. Team spirit has invariably been good at Derbyshire in my time and it helped make it fun to come to work.

Happily things started to pick up for both Derbyshire and myself. We reached the final of the Gillette Cup at Lord's in 1969, to give us a chance of winning a trophy for the first time since the championship in 1936. It had all been set up by a remarkable match at Chesterfield in the semi-final. In front of a full house, our old batting frailties were cruelly exposed and we crawled to 136 all out on a slow, spongy pitch. Sussex, with batsmen such as Ken Suttle, Jim Parks and Tony Greig in the side, had 60 overs in which to make 137. We bowled them out for 49, the lowest score at that time in the competition. Alan Ward and Harold Rhodes bowled 11 maidens in the first 14 overs and Peter Eyre finished them off with six for 18. After such a perform-ance we were counting the days until we played Yorkshire in the final, a Yorkshire team in a transitional phase, with the likes of Illingworth, Trueman and Binks gone. We reckoned without the special atmosphere of a cup final day at Lord's; quite simply we 'froze' and never did ourselves justice. We bowled well enough to restrict them to 219, but our batting never got out of second gear. Our captain, Derek Morgan, tried to do something about the slow start by putting Alan Ward up the order to number four, with orders to hit about him. Unfortunately Alan went in and played like a recognised batsman instead of a tail-end slogger and he took ages to make 17. We were all out for 150 and felt thoroughly chastened. We weren't the first side to 'freeze' on the big day, nor the last, and we again failed to do ourselves justice in 1978 when we reached the Benson and Hedges Cup final. It was to be 12 years before we hit the target with the NatWest Bank Trophy in 1981. One significant fact about that 1969 Derbyshire side – we lacked an overseas player. From 1968 onwards counties could sign an overseas star and that led to the likes of Kanhai, Sobers, Procter, Engineer, Barry Richards, Lloyd and McKenzie playing in county cricket. Yet Derbyshire were slow to get started and it was to be a couple of seasons before we signed the South African Chris Wilkins. For some reason we have never bought very wisely in the overseas market – at least not until John Wright and Peter Kirsten in the late 1970s – and, even then, we did not go for a fast bowler until Michael Holding in 1983. It always seemed obvious to me that the successful county sides had an overseas batsman, backed up by an overseas strike bowler, but above all the fast bowler was vital. It was to be 15 years before we got it right.

Two more postscripts to that Gillette Cup final. That night, I was drowning my sorrows with the players and wives in the Cricketers' Club when I was called to the phone. It was a tearful Colleen Rumsey, who asked about the whereabouts of her husband, Fred. Now Fred was a lovely lad, a fine fast bowler in his time and, at that stage, our commercial manager and public relations officer as well as an occasional player. On this occasion, Fred had taken his PRO duties too far and had stayed drinking in the Tavern after the game. Hence the call from Mrs Rumsey, who was alone in her hotel, sobbing her heart out. I had to leave our dinner party, hop into a taxi and go to console her while Fred got sozzled in St John's Wood! A perfect end to an imperfect day. A few hours later, and more embarrassment. Derek Morgan and I turned up at Bournemouth for our John Player League game against Hampshire to find that we were likely to have to play them on our own! The others had contrived to get lost on the way down from London and Derbyshire had just two players as Derek tossed the coin. The match had to start a few minutes late and one or two rollickings were handed out by the captain.

At least Derbyshire were beginning to attract some national publicity for (mostly) the right reasons and, as a result, I was getting a good press also. The powers-that-be at Lord's had obviously noted my name because I was selected several times for MCC against the champion county and the tourists. My mind went back to the day early in my career when my team-mate Bill Richardson had startled me with the remark, 'You know, Bob, I reckon you'll keep wicket for England one day.' That certainly never occurred to me at that early stage, but I must admit that, as the invitations from Lord's piled up, I began to harbour sneaking ambitions. I told myself that players at unfashionable counties such as Derbyshire have to be superb cricketers to get official recognition and that I would never be anything other than a good, solid pro. Yet Jim Parks and John Murray were getting no younger and, even though a youngster named Alan

Knott was making a good early impression, he might be just a shooting star. I looked around the counties, made a mental note of the opposition and dreamed my dreams. I bought an MCC diary and noted the forthcoming tours over the next few years.

First of all, I had to impress the bigwigs at Lord's in an important game and my chance came when I was picked for MCC against the 1969 West Indians. In the first over, a ball from John Snow passed Roy Fredericks down the leg side and I moved across to take it in conventional fashion. Suddenly it dipped and passed through me for four byes – it was the first time I had ever experienced a ball from a fast bowler deviate so much after it had passed the bat, and what a time for it to happen! Later on in the same match I was standing up to Basil D'Oliveira, with Garry Sobers batting; the ball came down the hill from the Nursery end, Sobers left a 'gate' between bat and pad and I felt sure the ball would hit the stumps. It went over the top of the off peg for another four byes, and all I could think of was 'Oh my God, did Gubby Allen or E. W. Swanton see that?'

I was selected by MCC later that year for my first overseas tour. It was a short tour to the Far East under the captaincy of Tony Lewis, with A. C. Smith player-manager, and it would include an unofficial Test in Ceylon, latterly Sri Lanka. It was a great thrill for me to go down to Lord's and experience the pre-tour ritual that I came to relish in later years – all that trying on of blazers and flannels, the posing for photographs, the dinner on the eve of departure. It was a delight and, if someone had told me that I would do this 11 more times before I retired 15 years later, I would have been astonished and gratified. This trip under Tony Lewis was basically a 'gin and tonic' tour to fly the flag to areas where not too many English players had been seen, and we had a good side, containing the likes of Geoff Boycott, Keith Fletcher, Geoff Arnold, Pat Pocock and John Hampshire. The steamy heat took some getting used to – after all I had never played abroad – but the standard of cricket was good, the hospitality tremendous and I loved it all. Presumably I can't have done too badly behind the stumps because A. C. Smith, a former England keeper himself, was very kind to me. It seemed a good omen as I entered my second decade in the professional game.

CHAPTER 3

MY FIRST ENGLAND TOUR

The first thing I did when I heard I was on my first full England tour was to stump up £7 and hand it over to my team-mates at Derby. I had taken bets from them that I would not be picked – and I have never been so happy to lose a wager! Everybody had been telling me that I was certain to go as understudy to Alan Knott, but I wouldn't have it; old habits die hard among the selectors and I felt that someone like Jim Parks or John Murray would still be there to give the squad some batting depth. If they believed that Murray (at 35) and Parks (39) were too old, I felt they might take a chance on young Roger Tolchard, who was a good batsman and kept wicket for Leicestershire, the county led by the England captain, Ray Illingworth. In any event, only five Derbyshire players had ever been on an England tour to Australia, so there was no point in denying we were an unfashionable county. Here again, the selectors caused a surprise in picking my colleague Alan Ward as well, so there was double cause for celebration in our dressing-room when the news was broken.

I had deliberately switched off from all the speculation in the previous weeks, because I felt my standards had to be maintained on behalf of the club that employed me. A tense wicketkeeper is no use to anyone other than the opposition, so I contented myself with the knowledge that I had done well on the MCC tour the previous winter, that A. C. Smith must have reported favourably on me to Lord's and that good, consistent form is the way to grab the attention of the selectors. In retrospect a July afternoon in 1970 must have helped my cause. We played Kent in a John Player League game and I dismissed three international batsmen while standing up to the seamers. I caught Mike Denness off Phil Russell – it bounced quickly off the shoulder of the bat and my reactions were quick – snared Asif Iqbal as he came down the pitch to Peter Eyre and then made a leg side stumping off Ian Buxton to get Colin Cowdrey. Colin was kind enough to say 'Well done, Bob' before he left the crease and I like to think that afternoon's work was in his thoughts when, as the England vice-captain for the Australian tour, he discussed me with the selectors a few weeks later.

I was overwhelmed with kindness from everyone after my selection. The press welcomed the news, pointing out that it was about time that the selectors reverted to the best two keepers and that I might push Alan Knott hard for the number one spot on tour. That was certainly my intention – after all, I was 29 and believed I was getting near to my peak. Much as I admired Alan, I felt it would be unfair to myself and to Ray Illingworth if I didn't think positively. As an unashamed traditionalist, I knew that the Australian tour was the big one for every England cricketer and I was very proud to learn that I was following in the footsteps of three Staffordshire men – S. F. Barnes, John Ikin and Ken Higgs. I would try my hardest to keep the county's flag flying.

Cathy and I had some experience of foreign travel to holiday spots like Majorca and Sardinia, but this was in a different league. I hope I haven't become blasé about travel, but I was never so excited again as I waited for my first trip to Australia. As a child, I had dreamed about going to the other side of the world and now it was happening; it had always astonished me that you could wake up in the morning in Sydney and it would be evening in Stoke. Now I would be able to see our great family friends – Valerie and Alan Clarke – who had emigrated out there in the mid-1960s. I assumed I would never see them again but the simple matter of keeping wicket to a decent standard had changed all that. And yet I had a scare just a week before the departure date, when I developed a terrible pain in my knee. I had been running on roads near to my home and the constant pounding on the hard surface had jarred my knee and given me fluid on it. I was examined by Stoke City's physiotherapist, he told me never to run again on hard surfaces and promised to keep quiet about it. He reassured me that the trouble would clear up soon, but I was taking no chances. On the flight out to Australia, I sat with my leg fully extended, with a crepe bandage from the top of the thigh to halfway down the calf. I didn't tell Ray Illingworth about it and I cursed that road running. Since then, I have always run on grass and never had any knee trouble.

Within a day or two of landing in Australia, the sore knee was fine and I was loving every minute of the tour. I couldn't get over standing in the middle of a city street at eight o'clock in the morning, with the temperature in the eighties! The scorching weather meant the wickets were ideal for batting, but the true bounce also made it easy for keeping wicket. I started well, managing one of my best leg-side stumpings, getting Derek Chadwick off the inslant bowling of Geoff Boycott, and I didn't concede a bye until 1,500 runs had been scored off the bat. Even then, it was an annoying way to lose my 100 per cent record – Bob Willis sprayed one down the leg side that swung tremendously after it passed the bat and I didn't get within three yards of it. It should have been four wides, but the umpire signalled four byes and I was upset that my copybook had been blotted in such an avoidable way. The fact that the umpire – a former keeper – apologised to me afterwards didn't really console me! It was important to have pride in my work, to keep pushing away at Alan Knott. After all, I was representing my country – albeit in state games – and I had sufficient ego to want the crowd and the opposition to think I had something of quality to offer.

Despite those sentiments I could not displace Alan Knott in that Australian series, nor did it ever look likely. I kept wicket well, but he followed suit; I batted well enough, but he did superbly, averaging 31 with the bat, besides his 24 dismissals. In the end, I managed just four first-class games in the 18 weeks of the Australian section of the tour. I played in all the up-country games and I wasn't the only one: John Hampshire and Don Wilson suggested we should design a tie for the ever-presents from those up-country skirmishes! I really couldn't complain, and it was some consolation when everyone kept telling me that I had helped to keep Alan Knott on his toes. Alan and I forged a strong mutual respect for each other on that tour – a feeling that has lasted to this day. We got along very well indeed and I was most touched by his gesture when the team was picked for the First Test against the Aussies – he came over to me and said, 'Bad luck, Bob, keep going.' He never failed to say the same thing on every similar occasion on our England tours together.

Ray Illingworth was terrific to me on that tour and overall a great captain for the side. He was easily the best captain I'd played under at that stage and, for England, only Mike Brearley rivals him in my career. Illy knew the game inside out, back to front and all of us had great confidence in him. You felt that if Illy was in charge, things would automatically work out for the best and in a very tense Test series he never lost control. He persuaded Geoff Boycott to play a few more shots on those beautiful batting wickets, with the result that Boycott batted better than at any other stage in my experience. He got through the moodiness of John Snow and somehow made him bowl his heart out as strike bowler. In each case, he made it clear to Snow and Boycott that an early plane home was the alternative if they didn't do what the captain asked. Illy fostered a great feeling of togetherness in the squad, so that even the reserves like myself, Don Wilson and John Hampshire were just as keyed up during the Tests as the 11 who were playing. We had some good solid professionals in that party – men like John Edrich, Brian Luckhurst, Basil D'Oliveira and Derek Underwood as well as the world-class performers – and Illy appealed to the best side of their professional make-up.

The captain also stood up for us when necessary. An example came when we thought we had been sold short over some sharp practice by the Australian Cricket Board. When the Melbourne Test was completely washed out, the Board wanted to organise a one-day international in its place – the first of its kind. Illy felt it was placing an additional strain on his players in a long series and said that we should be given extra cash for the game. We seriously discussed going on strike over the matter and the squad was solidly behind Illy. Eventually we were promised the extra money but that did nothing to smooth relations between the captain and our manager, David Clark. Now that was a chalk and-cheese affair if ever I saw one – Illy the tough Yorkshireman who wanted to win, Clark the gentleman-farmer from Kent who had been an amateur in the old days and longed to return to those supposedly chivalrous times. It was no secret that David Clark would rather Colin Cowdrey had been in charge – both Establishment figures, both colleagues from the same Kent team, with a rather romantic view of the modern game. As the tour progressed, the vice-captain distanced himself from Illy and David Clark barely concealed his distaste for the modern methods of playing Test cricket. After the first two Tests were drawn, the manager expressed the view to the press that a greater sense of urgency was needed. Not only did that ignore Illy's strategy – which was to hold firm in certain Tests and strike for victory on pitches that would help our spinners and John Snow – but the captain felt there was now a hostile presence in our camp. David Clark protested that his comments were not meant to be personal, but the damage was done as far as Illy was concerned. When we threatened to go on strike, the relationship got worse and one or two incidents on the field which were misconstrued by the media didn't help Illy either. The climax came when we returned to England with a 2-0 victory and were entertained at a victory dinner at Lord's where one gentleman remarked that it was a pity that our victory had been achieved at such a cost! I'm sure the tough Aussies would have been astonished at such a remark to a victorious team. They have never had any qualms about beating the living daylights out of the opposition, with whatever methods they can get away with.

I hasten to add that my relationship with David Clark was perfectly happy – as it always remained with Colin Cowdrey. Yet there was no doubt that the rest of us would have followed Ray Illingworth down any road he chose on that tour. He took all the flak on behalf of his players and simply demanded complete loyalty and professionalism in return. No problem. That last morning in the final Test at Sydney was a graphic example of Illy's control and skill: the Aussies were 123 for 5, with just 100 needed to win and Greg Chappell looking ominously good. In the first over, Illy drew him down the pitch, beat him in the flight and Knott stumped him – a classic piece of slow bowling. The rest of them disintegrated against Underwood and Illy, we won by 62 runs and the captain was chaired off the field.

Everything seemed to go right for us at crucial moments. Even the late selection of Bob Willis proved an inspiration. A month into the tour, he was sent for on the recommendation of his county team-mate John Edrich, after Alan Ward's ankle injury had ruled him out for the rest of the trip. I had only seen him once in county cricket and hadn't considered him anything special – yet he took some important wickets at a fair old speed, held some blinding catches in the gully and fitted in right away with everyone. As for Alan Ward, it was a great disappointment on a cricketing level, but even he enjoyed some consolation – he found a wife! While waiting for his flight home, Alan was drowning his sorrows with a spot of sun-bathing by the pool in Brisbane and he started chatting to a girl who was modelling bikinis. On the night that Alan flew back home, the girl rang me at the hotel and asked if she could come round and talk about my team-mate. It was clear that she and Alan thought a lot of each other and she asked me about Sheffield, his home town. I felt I had to give it to her straight and told her about the cold and the grime, but it was clear to me her mind was settled on going to England. By the time we returned to England in triumph, she was already there and their marriage has produced three lovely children. So at least Alan Ward got something worthwhile out of his ill-starred tour!

Apart from my frustrations on the playing side, I was very impressed by Australia. I accepted right from the start that we were in a different part of the world and there was no point in going on about Blighty. I made a lot of friends on that first tour and have subsequently enjoyed countless happy evenings in the homes of kind hosts – always a pleasant antidote to the loneliness of a hotel room. I felt homesick many times which was aggravated by the postal strike in Great Britain – luckily Cathy was working on the GPO switchboard in Stoke at the time and we managed one or two long phone calls. Yet she and I both knew that I had to make the best of the situation because of my professional ambitions; there was no point in moping around, wondering how Stoke City were getting on and thinking about a good old English pint by a roaring log fire. I was privileged to be out there, to be paid for the honour of representing English cricket. I wanted to get to know about the Australian make-up and that's how I acquired the nickname of 'Bob Chat' that has stayed with me ever since. Ray Illingworth had noticed how much I seemed to enjoy talking to non-cricketers at the various receptions we attended and he gave me the name. As far as I was concerned, it was simply a case of helping out our players who had been on their feet all day in the boiling heat under Test match pressure. I would have done nothing all that strenuous during the day and I saw it as my duty to give them a rest and fly the flag by chatting to as many people as possible. I saw it as part of my education as a tourist, and that continued to be my attitude long after I was established as England's number one. At countless receptions, too many current players slump together in the corner and go on about 'earbashers' without trying to talk to strangers. I usually made it my policy to chat to the wives of cricket administrators, who certainly didn't want to discuss cricket, and I found the exercise generally enjoyable. Eventually my 'Bob Chat' image became well known and on later tours I must admit I tried to keep up to that image – but I could never understand why so many international cricketers had a phobia about meeting nice, ordinary people who just happened to be standing around with a drink in their hands. I can honestly say that the bulk of strangers I have met at countless receptions over the years have been decent folk with no pretensions to 'earbashing'.

Having said that I did experience one or two cruel moments at those receptions on my first England tour. Invariably we had to don name-tags as we went into the room and inevitably I was less of a celebrity than John Snow, Basil D'Oliveira or Geoff Boycott. I recall several moments when someone would say, 'R. W. Taylor – and what do you do?' I must admit I had to bite my tongue on several occasions, and remember some sympathetic words from Graham McKenzie. 'You must really feel it about you and Knotty at these kind of occasions,' he said to me – and he was right. After all, I was there as one of England's 16 best cricketers and yet several guests did not know a thing at all about me. That used to hurt. A joke by Bill Lawry also got to me on that tour. He said, 'Bob, when I come back in the next life, I want to be England's second wicketkeeper on tour!' I told him he was talking nonsense because every professional sportsman worth his salt wants to play for his country. I suppose Bill – who was under great pressure at the time as Australia's captain – had seen me working out at the nets, then settling down to watch the cricket as twelfth man. He obviously thought it was a great swan but he didn't realise that I had to keep active to ward off my frustrations. Knotty was doing so superbly that I set myself to be the best twelfth man that an England touring party ever had. Apart from bowling in the nets to any batsman who wished to get some form back at my expense, I would mollycoddle them in the dressing-room. Whatever a player wanted, I would be meticulous in providing for them. Anyone not wishing to eat in the dining-room would have his place neatly laid out in the dressing-room, with enough elbow room to make him feel comfortable. I watched the play avidly for any signals from my fielders and I would scurry out there like a shot. Drinks at close of play were organised long in advance and absolutely nothing was left to chance.

All this was therapy to keep me involved. I knew that Knotty would not be toppled on this tour, but nobody would ever say that I sulked or that I held it against anyone. Of course, I looked forward to the off-duty hours, when I could get away from the cricket and sunbathe down by the beach to regain some sanity, but I was determined to be a 'team man' at all times. I never fielded during any of those Australian Tests, but that would have been preferable to sitting in the dressing-room, peering out at the action, wishing and hoping, while at the same time meaning no harm to Knotty. When I did manage to get onto the pitch – albeit as drinks waiter – I was set up beautifully by Doug Walters, the prime leg-puller among the Aussies. I brought out the drinks on the final day of the Perth Test in a basket and, as I was leaving the field, the handle came away and all the glasses came crashing down. Doug had loosened the handle and stood grinning at me as the umpire told the blushing England twelfth man to get a move on because he was holding up a Test match. As I made my flustered way back to the dressing-room, I plotted my revenge. I doctored Doug's drink with liver salts in the next session and it had the desired effect: he was on and off the field for the rest of the day! It must be said there was nothing in the game, which ended in a draw.

The atmosphere between the two sides was very friendly on that tour and has remained so throughout my time with England. The Aussies played it really hard on the pitch, but they were always the first to come into our dressing-room and share a few beers at close of play. I was very impressed with their administrators, particularly Sir Don Bradman. When we first arrived, he was there to meet us at the airport and he knew everyone by sight, even though hardly any of us had ever met him. He shook my hand and said, 'Welcome to Australia, Bob,' and his conversation revealed he had done his homework on me, as well as on all the others. In later years all the other top Australian administrators have been equally impressive on a personal level – men like Phil Ridings, Ray Steele, and Bob Parish all greeted us as if we were old friends and they made us feel very welcome. Quite a contrast to the rather stuffy atmosphere you get at Lord's; many times have I squirmed as a top official has struggled to place the overseas cricketer he is talking to, trying all the time to get on some common ground. The Aussies are streets ahead in this respect.

It was a tremendous thrill for me to meet someone of the stature of Sir Don Bradman, but an even greater treat was in store. I was introduced to the great Bertie Oldfield, one of the finest wicketkeepers of all time. Keith Andrew had been my source of introduction several years earlier when I had admired Keith's gloves. He told me he had got them from Bertie Oldfield's sports shop in Sydney, and I wrote off to him, asking to buy a pair. Sure enough, they arrived and they were superb – I took six catches in the first innings in which I wore them and, for good measure, didn't concede a bye in a total of over 300. Mr Oldfield also wrote me a charming letter of support, which impressed me very much, as he had no idea who I was. When we met, he was all that I expected him to be: a charming, dapper little man with impeccable manners and an air of gentle mastery. I spent a memorable evening talking cricket with him, and he gave me countless tips. When I returned to England, Mr Oldfield sent me another pair of his gloves, free of charge, with a long letter of encouragement and advice. He wrote about diet and fitness and added, 'Try hard to avoid hopping across in your effort to cover the delivery. Remember we can all learn if we are chosen as a wicketkeeper.' Then an interesting postscript to his letter: 'Claim as much rest as you can when visiting games against other county teams.' I thought it was wonderful that one of the all-time greats would put himself out for a Pommie. Even at 76 years of age, he still looked marvellously fit and trim. A year later, when I again toured Australia with the Rest of the World side, he invited me out to dinner with his family and I enjoyed another magical evening. When he died in 1976, I mourned one of the kindest, most impressive men I have ever met, a model to every cricketer of any era.

As I stood taking cocktails with Sir Don Bradman, discussing leg-spin bowling with the illustrious Clarrie Grimmett or talking over the finer points of wicketkeeping with Bertie Oldfield, it seemed a long way from Bignall End and that little fag-end of a kid with pads halfway up to his chest. Such evenings of nostalgia and enlightenment did much to ease the frustration of twelfth man duties. Little did I know that within a few weeks, I would be able to write 'Derbyshire and *England*' after my name.

The circumstances behind my first cap were unsatisfactory then and, years later, just as embarrassing now. I was selected as a consolation prize for being a good tourist: it was as simple as that. Alan Knott wasn't injured, he had been in magnificent form and did not deserve to be dropped. It also brought an end to his run of 28 consecutive Tests and I know he was rightly disappointed at the decision. As usual he was terrific to me, offering his congratulations and saying that I deserved it. That was nice of him, but it did dilute Test cricket in my eyes, even though my pleasure in playing for my country at last was immense. Don Wilson, who was also rewarded for his unselfish support work,

said to me, 'Well they can't take it away from you, Bob – Derbyshire and England,' and he was right. In years to come, it would
still be in *Wisden* – 'Taylor, R. W. 1: v NZ *1970.*'

The pitch at Christchurch was unrecognisable from the
belters that we had enjoyed in Australia. At first sight, it looked
like a ploughed field. No wonder: Canterbury played rugby on
it during the winter and there had been a lot of rain lately, which
churned up the outfield. It looked tailor-made for our three
spinners and, sure enough, Derek Underwood took 12 wickets
in the match as we won by eight wickets. I was pleased with my
keeping and the way I adapted to the overcast conditions and
deviation of the ball after the harsh glare of Australia. The
environment and playing conditions were more like Derby than
the Southern Hemisphere, as I realised when Ray Illingworth
pitched one just outside Glenn Turner's off stump and it shot
past my left shoulder for four byes on the leg side! Within a few
minutes of the match, I had snaffled the first two catches of my
Test career off Ken Shuttleworth – the first was Bruce Murray,
who followed a bouncer and gloved an easy catch to me. That
settled me down and I really enjoyed keeping to Illy and Underwood. They were so accurate, so relentless that the New Zealanders were never going to get on top of them.

When I batted – in the exalted position of number seven, I
might add – I was adjudged out by, of all people, the former
Derbyshire batsman, Charlie Elliott. Charlie, a highly respected
Test umpire, was over there on a scholarship and was invited to
stand as a guest umpire in the First Test match. I played forward
to Hedley Howarth, missed it, but kept my back foot anchored
in the crease. I heard a shout of 'well bowled', I looked up and
around and saw Charlie standing at square leg with his finger up.
Stumped Wadsworth bowled Howarth 4. The first and last time
I have been stumped on the forward defensive in a Test!

So my brief flirtation with the real thing was over. Knotty
came back for the Second Test at Auckland, to keep brilliantly
and score 101 and 96 – point proved, I fear. It was some satisfaction to me that my presence in the team had clearly geed him up
and, like a great Test match performer, he delivered the goods
next time around. There was still no doubt in my mind who was
the number one. Yet I had done myself justice behind the stumps,
even if I shouldn't really have been there. I was conscious of a
slight feeling of disappointment about my Test debut – perhaps
it was the small crowd, the poor pitch, the sharp contrast between

the tension of Sydney and the fight for the Ashes. I hadn't been nervous the night before my debut – such feelings came later in my Test career when I was under pressure to maintain my standards – and, given the circumstances of my selection, it had all seemed an adventure, a little unreal.

It was disappointing that my appearance at Christchurch didn't entitle me to wear an England cap. In those days, they were MCC rather than England tours and, although we were all kitted out with that splendid MCC blazer, we didn't get the cap with the three lions and crown for overseas Tests. That changed on the 1977–78 tour of Pakistan and New Zealand, when England caps began to be awarded, wherever they were won. As soon as the first day's play had ended in the First Test at Lahore, I telexed Cathy, asking her to contact Simpson's of Piccadilly about the England blazer I was now entitled to wear. I wanted it to be ready for me when I returned from my first tour as England's number one. I was so anxious to claim my England blazer at last that I didn't want to wait a single day longer than necessary. So, seven years on from my Test debut, I could wear my England cap and blazer with pride. I had something tangible to show for representing my country.

Five months after the tour began, we were home. I picked up £900 for that first England trip, compared with £10,000 for subsequent, much shorter tours. Yet I would have gone for nothing. It had been a tremendous thrill to experience that special brand of camaraderie that comes on a tour when you are up against it, facing the toughest opposition, and you pull through. I had played only 26 days of cricket during those five months, but the experience had been fantastic, despite the frustrations. I had witnessed at first hand the tremendous pressures of an Ashes series and seen what it could do to the most seasoned of players. Ray Illingworth had demonstrated the importance of strong leadership and we would have gone through brick walls for him. As for myself, I was happy with my form behind the stumps – 19 victims in just five first-class games, plus a batting average of 16 – but Knotty's average of almost 45, plus some brilliant keeping, was a total vindication of his selection ahead of me. Many critics said some very kind things about me – in fact Barry Jarman, the former Australian wicketkeeper, even suggested that the authorities should try to persuade me to emigrate out there and play for them! I thought that was very amusing, but underlying the fatuous suggestion was an acknowledgement from an ex-Test keeper that I wasn't the worst glove-man that he had seen. I needed such praise to keep going, to give me hope that someday I would be England's number one. I did not realise that such a dream was almost seven years away and that it would take the intervention of an Australian millionaire to accomplish it.

CHAPTER 4

THE BRIDESMAID TO ALAN KNOTT

The next six years were to be frustrating and occasionally despairing ones for me. I just couldn't topple Alan Knott from his position as England's number one, nor did I deserve to. Quite simply he was the best around and whenever it looked as if I might get close to him, he drew away, like an Olympic runner coming round the last bend. A case in point was that first English season after the Australian tour, when I made a conscious effort to get more runs. I had seen the virtue of concentration at first hand from the likes of Boycott, Edrich and Luckhurst and I battled hard for Derbyshire to get over 600 runs with an average of almost 25, including three fifties. Knotty topped that with 1,200 runs, three hundreds (including one in the Tests) and more dismissals in one game less than me. It was small consolation to read in the press that England were so lucky to have two such skilful keepers and that I would have played for any other Test country.

At least I was still in the selectors' minds and I just kept plugging away, doing my best for Derbyshire. After all, they were my employers and I owed it to them and to myself to maintain my high standards. The county grapevine would soon get working if my form had deteriorated during those years in the wilderness and the news would have filtered through to the selectors. My reward was to go on two more England tours as Alan's understudy and I had to pull out of another one because of an ear infection. Even then, I couldn't get rid of the feeling that I was the bridesmaid and that was underlined when Alan dropped out of the tour to Australia in 1971–72 with the Rest of the World side. I was asked to take his place, but it was made clear that the number one would be Farokh Engineer, the Indian who played for Lancashire. It was necessary to swallow my pride and rationalise the situation: I wasn't the original choice, but I owed it to myself to go back to Australia and get some more experience at a high level. After all, I would be standing up to the likes of Bishan Bedi, Intikhab Alam and Norman Gifford and that sounded a very enjoyable prospect. It would mean more than three months away from home, but it was all good experience with a team containing the likes of Sobers, Gavaskar, Kanhai, the Pollock brothers, Clive Lloyd and Zaheer Abbas. In fact it was much closer to a genuine Rest of the World side than other tour organisers have managed, and I agreed to go. It was important to remain in the public eye, to be appreciated by a wider audience and to topple Engineer from his number one spot. Professional pride demanded that I got into the team and I managed it for the last unofficial Test of the series. I picked up five catches in the game, including a very good one to get Greg Chappell – an inside edge off a googly from Intikhab. In seven games, I managed 24 victims and was pleased with my performance.

Around that time, I was trying to widen my skills in keeping to the spinner – Derbyshire still relied predominantly on seamers – and it was a tremendous thrill to keep to Bedi and Intikhab. Bedi was a beautiful bowler – it was almost as if he had the ball on a piece of string, holding it back, playing it out, but the batsman was never quite there. Great players would hit him for six, and Bishan would join in the applause, giving the batsman a long, lingering look. Invariably, the ball would be hit straight up in the air shortly afterwards as Bishan lulled the batsman into a feeling of over-confidence. Intikhab wasn't as big a spinner as Bedi, nor such a superb 'flight' bowler, but he was uncommonly accurate for a leg-spinner, a great thinker with good variety and a wonderful trier. The pleasure in keeping to those two has only been surpassed once in my career – in 1973 when I played at Eastbourne for D. H. Robins' XI against the West Indians. That day, Mushtaq Mohammad added his leggies and googlies to those of Intikhab and the wiles of Bedi and I had the time of my life, standing up to those three.

As one would expect, the quality of cricket on that tour was exceptionally high. To win 2-1, we really had to try our hardest against an Australian side coming out of the doldrums under the aggressive leadership of Ian Chappell. He was beginning to forge a strong side around the batting of himself and his brother, Greg, the improved wicketkeeping of Rodney Marsh, the swing bowling of Bob Massie and the superb fast bowling of Dennis

Lillee. Just a year on from their defeat by England, these Aussies looked a formidable outfit and so it proved. They proceeded to dominate world cricket for the next five years until Kerry Packer came along.

It had done me no harm at all to go on the tour and to forget that I was only there as a stand-in for Knotty. Luckily Doug Insole and 'Gubby' Allen, two of the most influential figures at Lord's, thought so too. I happened to bump into them at my hotel in Adelaide after that final game and they said, 'Well done – you kept wicket very well.' They were obviously over in Australia on official business and it was fortunate for me that it coincided with the only game I played during that series. At least it meant I was still in the picture at Lord's, when the selectors sat down to discuss England teams and tour parties. So it proved a few months later: I was selected, along with Alan Knott, for the tour to India and Pakistan. I was really looking forward to that tour – we were taking spinners of the calibre of Pat Pocock, Derek Underwood and Jack Birkenshaw and I would be able to see the likes of Bedi, Chandrasekhar and Prasanna at first hand. There was even the chance that I might play a Test or two as a batsman if Knotty maintained his brilliance; Bernard Thomas, the England physio-therapist, had told me that it was to be a long, wearying tour with the risk of illness. It could be a case of England sending out the only 11 fit men they had, and I was determined to be one of them. An England 'cap' is an England 'cap', whether or not the wicketkeeping pads are donned.

Imagine my disappointment, when a couple of weeks before departure, I was ruled out of the tour with an ear infection. The doctor appointed by Lord's said I needed a mastoid operation and that I couldn't possibly go to the Indian sub-continent, where the risk of infection was far greater. I could have cried and the consoling words from the doctor ('it's better in the long run, you'll thank me for this') were useless. As a boy, I'd suffered from sore ears and my mother sometimes sent me to school with a balaclava on my head, and a hot onion stuffed between the balaclava and my left ear. Mum used to warm the onion by the fire and it retained the heat, acting like a hot water bottle. I thought no more of it until that day in a St John's Wood surgery in 1972, when the doctor asked me about my ears. I was suffering from a slight head cold and was discharging some fluid in my ear and he spotted the trouble right away. In hindsight he was quite correct – it could have lead to some deafness – and he often apologised when examining me for subsequent tours. To make matters worse, my replacement – Roger Tolchard – was given all my gear. He was the same size as me, so he took the MCC blazer, and even my travelling bag bearing the initials 'R.W.T.'. Three of my intended colleagues on that tour rang up to commiserate – Barry Wood, Mike Denness and Alan Knott, a typical gesture from Knotty. Their words, though sincere, were wasted on me, because I was feeling sorry for myself. I almost burst into tears one day in a specialist's waiting-room, as I sat there preparing for another check-up. I picked up a magazine and my eyes chanced upon some words by Patience Strong that seemed to sum up what was needed. 'There are intervals in life. The show can't run non-stop. In between the acts there comes a pause. The curtain drops. Intervals there have to be; accept them. Face the facts. Wisely use the quiet times that come between the acts.' Those words were so appropriate at the time for me – I just had to shake myself out of my desolation. After two successive winter tours, I was to spend the next few months at home. That was never any personal hardship to a family man like me, but I had to shelve my professional frustrations. I had enjoyed the taste of representative cricket and it would still be there if I was good enough. At least the ear operation meant I'd always be able to hear the snicks in my old age!

I was fit and refreshed for the 1973 season – my benefit year, when so many kind people worked very hard on my behalf. Just under £7,000 may not seem a large amount a decade later, but it helped give me a slice of the security that every sportsman needs. That security was fostered by the England selectors that summer, because they picked me for the one-day internationals against West Indies, and I was pleased with my display. At Headingley, I stumped Alvin Kallicharran: Derek Underwood, bowling round the wicket, sent one down the leg side, Alvin missed a full-length delivery and I took it ankle-high to stump him. Geoff Boycott walked over to me and said, 'That's got you on the trip to West Indies,' and he was right.

The 1973–74 tour of West Indies was the only time I came near to deposing Alan Knott. I didn't get a first-class game until after our heavy defeat in the First Test and I made it count. I kept wicket well and made 65 in good style – those wickets were very flat out there! Knotty had been struggling with the bat and he wasn't quite up to the mark behind the stumps either. I don't know what was going on in the minds of Mike Denness, the captain, and the other selectors, but I felt I had a real chance. They gave him another go in the next Test and he picked up form. Knotty ended the series with a batting average of 45 and, the longer it went on, the more he kept wicket as superbly as ever. Somehow the combined efforts of Amiss, Boycott, Knott and Greig managed to stage a recovery and we got away with a 1-1 series draw, which was a little harsh on West Indies. There was no doubt that Knotty's supreme Test match temperament was vital during those tense games and, yet again, he had come through. I ended up with just three first-class appearances on a tour that lasted more than three months. So near and yet so far.

My performances on the tours must have impressed the right judges, though, because I never felt I was out of the selectors' considerations in that period. During the 1974 season, Mike Denness would seek me out for an encouraging chat whenever our paths crossed; he made it clear that, as long as he was England captain, I would be on tour with him and first reserve to Knotty. Colin Cowdrey was his usual thoughtful self to me also. I was now 33 and had rationalised the situation. I just had to keep going, to provide my own motivation and not get dragged down by Derbyshire's poor performances. In 1974, we finished bottom of the championship table for the second season running; in four seasons, we had been last three times and sixteenth. The club was desperately short of money and, not surprisingly, membership remained scanty. On the face of it, a nightmare situation for someone like me who had ambitions to better himself as a player. Yet I was never unhappy with my lot at Derby; team spirit was always excellent and we had some fun, despite the depressing performances on the field. I suppose I could have made some comments in the press about my England prospects being damaged by playing for a poor side, but that was never my style. No one ever approached me and I never took the initiative with another county. It was handy to live an hour's drive away from the ground: on the way home, I could unwind mentally and then switch off from cricket as I walked through the door to my family. Besides, I never forgot what Derbyshire had given me – confidence in my own ability, the chance to play cricket for a living and to travel the world at someone else's expense.

Nevertheless, I needed to set myself goals to keep the motivation going. By the mid-1970s I had started to take a sudden interest in my career tally of dismissals. I reached my 1,000th dismissal in catching John Abrahams at Old Trafford in 1975 and started to think about my eventual total when I retired. I had no idea I was on 999 when I took the catch – the press have always been very good at telling me about the various milestones I have just passed – but I settled down one day with *Wisden* and looked at the others who had beaten my total. Herbert Strudwick was way out there with 1,493 dismissals but it looked as if J. T. Murray would pass that before he retired. He did, ending up with 1,527. I calculated that to get anywhere near that, I would need to play at least another eight seasons: my seasonal tally was averaging about 60 now, due to less first-class cricket, the lack of penetration by Derbyshire's bowlers and flatter wickets. The projection was spot on – I passed J. T. Murray's record in 1982. I hope such calculations don't seem too selfish and cold-blooded; it was simply a case of finding one more way of keeping my standards up to the mark. I've never been the Geoffrey Boycott of wicket-keepers, but at that stage I had been in the game for 13 years and I wanted to avoid getting stale at all costs. I dearly wanted to play for England again and I reasoned that the only way to achieve that was by consistency. Surely Alan Knott would slip from his high standards one of these days?

There was no sign of that on our next tour together – to Australia in 1974–75. Although we were slaughtered 4-1 by a superior bowling side, Alan again did splendidly. He was one of the few batsmen who worked out a satisfactory way to play the steep bounce of Jeff Thomson, the magnificent variety of Dennis Lillee, the nagging accuracy of Max Walker all this on green, under-prepared wickets, Thomson bowled at the speed of light from a remarkable, slinging action and somehow he could get the ball to rear up off short of a length. We lacked genuine, hostile pace at both ends and our batsmen were overwhelmed. I don't believe any other batsman left at home would have coped any better and that's why Alan Knott was so admirable. His keeping was as good as ever and he also scored a century and three fifties in that series against an irresistible bowling combination, backed up by fabulous catching and dynamic captaincy. I knew early on that I hadn't a hope of batting as well against that stuff and I slackened off perceptibly. This was the one tour I shared with Knotty when I gave less than 100 per cent to my duties as twelfth man and general supporting reserve. It suddenly hit me that the novelty of England tours was beginning to wear off, that I was getting nowhere. My rival was the best in the world and no matter how dedicated I would end up being the dogsbody, the one who gets things organised for the lucky ones who play. Time dragged; I got fed up of doing the same old things, of standing in for others who couldn't be bothered with twelfth man duty. Bill Lawry's quote of 1971 kept coming back to me and it was difficult to be philosophical when your team is getting thrashed and you cannot even get into that demoralised side. I knew there would be no consolation prize for me in the New Zealand leg of the tour – nor did I want a repetition of Christchurch 1971. Knotty had to stay in on merit. I got particularly homesick when several of the players' wives came out to join their husbands – to make it worse, their children came too. I felt it was wrong to ask Test players to perform at their best against Lillee and Thomson the following morning when they'd been up during the night with their small children – and I'm sure our manager, Alec Bedser, felt the same way. Our hotels were turned into kindergartens and, although none of the family men missed practice or arrived late for anything, it was clear that they were a little distracted by their children's presence. It was particularly galling for me because I was about the only one who wasn't in contention for a game. I could have had my two children and Cathy out there all the time, for all the difference it would have made to my performances on the field of play. It was, however, out of the question – the others had been picking up £200 a Test for several years, while I had managed just one Test appearance. On top of that, we had lost over £500 with the collapse of the Court Line holiday business in August 1974; although we got some of the money back, it would never have been enough to afford a trip to Australia for Cathy.

So I drifted along during that tour, part of the set-up, yet apart from it. Mike Denness was a little more assertive as captain than he had been in West Indies, but he lacked powers of motivation and I sensed that one or two of the senior players lacked respect for him. We were ripe for plucking by the powerful Australian side and all our heads dropped a little. I know mine did: I hope my disenchantment didn't stand out that much, but I did find it hard to keep up appearances. There was so little cricket outside the six-Test series that I was hardly over-employed. It was four years later that I learned that my disenchantment had been visible. Bernard Thomas pointed this out to me when I mentioned during our next tour of Australia that John Lever was looking slapdash and uncaring because he was out of the Test side – he said 'You went the same way the last time we were here.'

That shocked me because I thought I had kept my frustration to myself. On such a long tour, I suppose it's inevitable that members of the party notice changes in personality. I hope my support for the lads wasn't noticeably cooler.

At least my three tours as deputy to Alan Knott allowed me to appreciate his worth. Over the years, people have kindly remarked that I was superior to him as a gloveman, but I don't really swallow that one. I will always put my boyhood idol, Keith Andrew, at the top of the tree, but Knotty was the best performer in Tests. He had a beautiful pair of hands, great anticipation and terrific concentration. Quite apart from his batting, he would have been an automatic choice as England keeper at any period in the game's history. His consistency over a long period of time was tremendous and, although he occasionally suffered some knocks in the press, I think that was due to a fondness to have a go at an institution, just because he'd been there a long time. He was particularly admirable on tour, because he never really wanted to leave his home and family during the winter. Alan would get more homesick than any of us, and frequently would retire to his hotel room to watch television or write letters. Perhaps he should have done more to lift morale on his later England tours – after all, he was an experienced, world-class performer – and perhaps he overdid the obsession with health foods and clean cutlery abroad. Yet that stemmed from Alan's dedication, his determination to be at his peak when stepping onto the pitch. He knew the best ways to tune up for the big days and no one can ever say he didn't give great value.

It was often said that we were different in our wicketkeeping styles, but I didn't really think so. Alan was perhaps a little more flamboyant but he had to dive more than me because he wasn't as supple. This may surprise those who conjure up visions of Knotty leaping around like a salmon, but he had a spinal deficiency that would sometimes give him pain and restrict his movements. Hence all those stretching exercises between deliveries; he realised he had to keep limbering up, to be ready to move at speed. That is why he had to dive more – I would have been able to get the ball more easily because I have never suffered muscle problems. Our gift of anticipation was the same, but I could usually get two hands to the ball, while Alan would lack that split second athleticism, so he had to rely on a one-handed take. If he had been as supple as me, he wouldn't have needed to leap around. That was always particularly evident in our work down the leg side, where I think I picked up the line of the ball a fraction quicker. Alan would leave it just a shade later than me before he would commit himself.

I envied him his long partnership with Derek Underwood – a great bowler to work with because of his accuracy and determination. Throughout our county days, Alan invariably had the edge on me in terms of practice against the spinners; I've always maintained that the true test of a keeper comes when he stands up to spin bowling. Given his mastery, it must have seemed odd that Alan chose to stand back to medium-pacers like Tony Greig and Bob Woolmer; for me, it was always a test of skill to stand up to those types. I would only stand back to medium-pace on the rare occasions when we were into the final minutes of a limited-overs match when the tail-enders were in, the match was very tight and we couldn't afford to concede any byes from a freakish bounce. Alan would usually adopt that attitude throughout a limited-overs match, taking the reasonable view that every run was vital and that some byes are avoidable. For my part, I felt that a batsman using his feet or scuffing up the pitch with his spikes should be intimidated by a keeper standing up to the wicket, so that he gets worried about being stumped. Who is to say one or the other was right? I will say that Alan wasn't always standing back through his own free will: some bowlers of medium-pace prefer to see the keeper back, in case he sends down a wild delivery or the batsman snicks the ball hard and fast. This happened to me in my early days at Derbyshire, with Ian Buxton and Derek Morgan, and again on the MCC tour of the Far East in 1969–70. Don Shepherd, Glamorgan's experienced off-cutter, told me then that his county keeper, David Evans, always stood back to him and he preferred it that way. I tried standing up to him early on, with satisfactory results, but Don wasn't happy about it and in the end he drove me back. It just shows that the wicketkeeper doesn't always have the final say on where he stands.

Alan and I got on very well right from the start. He knew that I wanted to knock him off his perch, I knew that he would do his utmost to stay number one, but that never harmed our friendship. We were good for each other – Alan knew that I wouldn't let England down if I got in and I was aware of just how good he was by studying him at close quarters under the pressures of a Test. I always appreciated his words of commiseration whenever the Test team was announced on tour and I subsequently tried to be equally helpful to my understudies when I was the regular keeper. We have both been put under pressure to say something controversial about the other during our rivalry but there was nothing to say on that score; we liked and respected each other, and always looked forward to a natter during a county season. On our first tour together, he played a splendid practical joke on me: I was twelfth man with our side batting, there was no urgent need for me to watch every ball, so I went for a snooze under a shady tree. I was still dozing when the drinks interval came around, so Alan donned my blazer, sprinkled some talcum powder on his hair to give him the Taylor streak and imitated my walk on the way out to the middle. It got a great laugh as I woke up with a startled cry of embarrassment, and it only underlined our friendship.

I read somewhere once that Alan believed I was head and shoulders above him as a wicketkeeper pure and simple. I don't believe that and I believe he was just being kind to me, because he knew the frustrations I was experiencing as his perennial understudy. I do believe, though, that his batting was the main reason why he always got the nod over me. More than 4,000 runs at an average of 32 and five Test hundreds in addition to no less than 269 dismissals – a fantastic allround performance that will stand the test of time. No amount of consoling words to me can alter the fact that Alan delivered the goods consistently at the highest level. I could never match his audacious strokeplay, his ability to change the course of a game at number six or seven in the batting order. My strengths as a batsman lay in sensible support of a strokemaker, in the ability to use my good temperament to hang around and blunt the bowling – several classes below Knotty, in other words.

I never bore the slightest animosity towards Knotty – not even when he displaced me in the England side in 1980 and again in 1981. I didn't blame him for answering the call – at £1,500 a Test he would have been stupid to turn it down – but I do blame the selectors for a lack of principle. Knotty had made it clear that he didn't wish to tour again, so it looked as if he could pick and choose his moments to play for England. I know that Alan didn't see it that way, but I feel the selectors should have stood by someone who would gladly have gone anywhere in the world to play for his country.

By that time, I was getting used to disappointments at the hands of the selectors. The first real bombshell came in 1976, when I wasn't picked for the tour of India and Australia. Roger Tolchard went as understudy to Knotty and I would be lying if I said it didn't hurt. No offence to Roger, but no one would seriously claim he was high on the list of top wicketkeepers in the country, and it was clear that batting considerations were a vital part of that decision. In the end, he played as a batsman in four of the Indian Tests, and scored one valuable fifty, but it was an apt condemnation of the quality of England's batting that they had to play a second keeper as a number five batsman. When I heard that I hadn't been picked for that tour, I told Cathy to throw away my touring gear; I was convinced I was finished with England. I was now 35, Knotty was five years younger and it seemed that all my time spent as his understudy had been wasted. Christchurch 1971 was to be my only taste of the real stuff. I had joined that select band of Englishmen who had played just once for their country. I was disappointed on all sorts of levels – my Derbyshire team-mate Geoff Miller was going on his first England tour and I would have loved to keep to his off-spin and the wiles of Derek Underwood. The Indian continent attracted me as a place to visit, yet, four years after dropping out of Tony Lewis's tour, I had missed out again. On top of all that, the Centenary Test at Melbourne was to climax the tour in March and I would dearly have loved to be there. I knew that qualification for the free trip was to have played once against Australia, but I hoped against hope that the places of those who dropped out might be filled by the likes of me – having made three trips to Australia, two of them with England and one with a Rest of the World side under the auspices of the Australian Cricket Board. It was a forlorn hope and I can understand why the sponsors couldn't bend the rules to suit a traditionalist who would have revelled in the nostalgia of the occasion.

My disenchantment with the selectors deepened when the England lads returned from that tour. I was told by one of the press party that the selectors had confirmed that I was to be flown out in an emergency if anything happened to Knotty. If this was indeed the case, I certainly knew nothing about it, otherwise I would have kept myself fit throughout the winter of 1976–77, ready to fly out at a moment's notice. This annoyed me, because I would not have done myself justice if called upon and no one at Lord's bothered to tell me about the arrangement. They should have paid me a retainer to maintain peak fitness, but it seemed to me as if I was just at their beck and call. What is the point in having someone as standby, thousands of miles away, when the player is unaware of it? I am glad to say that things have been improved in that direction for subsequent tours – several players are now paid to keep themselves ready for a sudden trip – but that oversight did nothing to improve my sense of disillusionment in the spring of 1977. I genuinely felt I ought to have been treated with more respect, after proving to be a good tourist in previous years.

Unknown to me, events were moving at such a pace off the field that my grievance with Lord's was soon to become irrelevant. Kerry Packer was about to unveil his plans that would consign Alan Knott to the arms of World Series Cricket and deliver me into the position of England's number one wicket-keeper. I would turn out to be grateful to Cathy for ignoring my bitter words in the autumn of 1976. For a couple of years at least, the friendly rivalry between Alan Knott and Bob Taylor was to be placed in the pending tray.

CAPTAIN OF DERBYSHIRE

During the time I was trying to topple Knotty, I experienced a fascinating year in which I tried to come to terms with keeping wicket and captaincy. In the end, I had to give it up because I was worried that it would affect my form behind the stumps, but it was an enjoyable experience that only underlined that you are never too old to learn a few new cricketing tricks.

The call came in May 1975 when we were emphatically in the doldrums. Despite a clutch of Test players on our books, we couldn't get out of the basement area of the championship and our prospects looked gloomier, year after year. Brian Bolus, our experienced captain, was under pressure as soon as we were eliminated from the northern section of the Benson and Hedges Cup in 1975 – he also had business worries that were affecting his batting and it was clear that the captaincy was getting him down. Brian asked to be relieved of the job in the hope that he would regain his form and start enjoying his game again, and the committee put it to me that I should succeed him. I suppose that, as senior professional, I was a logical choice but I was concerned that it might affect how I kept wicket. To me that was where my main value to my employers lay, and I didn't want to disrupt my consistency. On reflection, I had noticed that experienced keepers like Alan Smith, Brian Taylor and Harold Stephenson had all combined the two jobs well at county level, so I agreed to do it until the end of the season and take it from there.

My first task was an unenviable one: to drop Brian Bolus. The selection committee for my first game agreed that Brian needed a rest and it was my painful task to tell a former captain and England batsman that he was out. He was far from happy, but I am glad to say that his form picked up drastically later in the season and he ended top of the batting averages. Initially, I was concerned with the confidence of my players. Having been on several England tours, I could see how vital it was to have the right attitude. It wasn't just talent that made someone an England player, but concentration, determination and the consistent use of that talent into an effective performance. I tried to tell our lads that they were as good as the rest, to rid themselves of the defeatism that stems from being whipping boys for other counties over recent seasons. It doesn't matter how long you have been playing with a bunch of grand lads – you won't really get to know them until you have to captain the side. I tried to talk to them individually, to point out the good points in their cricket and to use my experience to point them in the right direction.

It was gratifying to see an improvement in morale and playing performance in that 1975 season, although I wasn't fooled : teams invariably pick up under a new captain for a short period, then revert to their bad old ways. Nevertheless we won five championship games, reached a mid-table position in the John Player League and got to the semi-finals of the Gillette Cup. My own form didn't suffer under the responsibility – I scored over 700 first-class runs and made more dismissals than at any time since 1965. I had told the committee that the mental pressures of captaincy in so many different competitions worried me, that the side would be harmed if my standards dropped behind the stumps, but there was no sign of that in that first season of my leadership. I readily agreed to continue with the job.

Things started to go wrong early in the 1976 season. It was a combination of factors, some more important than others. Again we were eliminated early in the Benson and Hedges Cup, when it was vital to give the players and members an early-season boost to prove we had turned the corner. All of a sudden, I found myself weighed down with petty problems that were sapping my concentration when I got on the field. The saga of the team bus got me down, for example. It all stemmed from a well-meaning attempt by our new chairman, George Hughes, to save the club some money. Mr Hughes was head of a coach-building company and he provided a coach to take all of us to away matches; it was equipped with a television, stereo, bar, reclining seats and a card table. The idea was to save on travelling expenses instead of going in separate cars and we agreed to try it out, because we were well aware that the club was short of cash. From the start, the coach was a disaster – the seats didn't recline, the television fell down off its raised area, we couldn't hear the stereo for the engine noise and it only travelled at about forty miles an hour. Sometimes we were even overtaken uphill by cyclists! When we stayed at a hotel for an away match, I had to run around getting everybody rounded up for the coach's departure to get to the ground – otherwise they had to take a taxi. On the way home, it was a nightmare: the drinkers would want to stop at a pub while the teetotallers stayed in the coach, waiting to get started. When we got back to Derby, we all had to wend our way back home in our own cars – for someone like me, that added another hour to the journey. On top of all that, we were sick of the sight of each other; in a long season, you need an occasional break from your team-mates, yet we were cooped up all day long in the dressing-room, then in this coach. That was very relevant to our disappointing performances in the field, in my opinion. I got the lads to vote to get rid of the bus when I heard that instead of saving the club £5,000 it was only saving £800. I told the committee that such a measure wasn't worth destroying team spirit for the sake of just £800.

After a time, I began to get depressed. I seemed to be telling someone off all the time; the rollickings were well deserved and I believe the players concerned respected me and accepted my complaints, but it seemed as if I was always getting at someone. My standards were higher than those of some of my team-mates and so I felt it was right to hand out lectures, but I found myself thinking, 'Listen to yourself – is that really you talking like that?' On top of that, my son, Mark was about 13 at the time and I was ticking him off a lot at home for the kind of misdemeanours all kids do at that age – but it didn't improve my mood. For the first time in my career, I found myself arriving at the ground not bothered about playing. That wasn't like me at all, and I was determined to snap out of my mood. I asked the lads for a vote of confidence and they gave it readily. Yet I only lasted another six weeks before resigning. I realised that temperamentally, I'm not a captain – I'm a number two, a foreman who gets people moving on the pitch when we are fielding, a back-up to the captain. It was clear to me that my wicketkeeping was sure to be affected if I stayed in the job any longer. Close observers of our team maintained that my standards hadn't slipped at all, but I felt there were too many details on and off the field that were beginning to sap my concentration. That came home to me one day when Phil Sharpe, in his usual first-slip position, suggested a tactical change to me. He made the suggestion just as the bowler was coming in – not Phil's fault, he spoke on the spur of the moment and I wasn't ready for the delivery. As luck would have it, the batsman got a nick and I dropped a straightforward outside edge. That wouldn't have happened if I hadn't been captain that day.

I felt a strong sense of failure that I could not see the job through, but it was obvious to me that my primary value to Derbyshire was as a wicketkeeper who set himself the highest standards. I took things to heart, feeling I had failed, when there was no reason to be so sensitive. The case of Fred Swarbrook was a big test of my captaincy: for some reason, Fred couldn't bowl his left-arm spin out in the middle for a period and it got to all of us. He was fine in the nets, but went to pieces during the game. We would lose matches that we ought to have won on turning wickets after winning the toss and batting first – and Fred would burst into tears in the dressing-room because he knew he should have bowled the sides out in such conditions. I had to exercise my authority as captain and make him bowl in matches, even though I realised he was going through a personal hell. Fred was never really the same again – he left the staff in 1979. He was only 29, with his best years still ahead of him as a spinner, but he had lost it. It was during my captaincy that he began to deteriorate psychologically and I have often wondered if I should have handled him differently.

As a captain, I think I erred on the side of caution. Perhaps it was due to being brought up in a hard school, where you gave the opposition nothing; perhaps I was worried that the team was still not confident enough to go all out for victory. Certainly, Eddie Barlow and Kim Barnett – who have subsequently captained Derbyshire – were bolder leaders. In my defence though, I think I was tactically sound, reading the wickets and the bowling permutations well enough. The main bugbear was that the Derbyshire captaincy had stopped me looking forward to going to work. The experience was good for me, giving me fresh insights into my profession but I can honestly state that a keeper should be captain only on the rarest of occasions in first-class cricket. The mental strains of keeping wicket are just too much to be able to spend the time worrying about the nuts and bolts. The captain should be detached and analytical, while it is the keeper's job to bawl out fielders and slap bowlers on the backside, telling them they're bowling well. I know from bitter experience that whenever I've kept wicket badly it's been due to one of three things – I've lost my concentration, I've got up too quickly from the usual crouched position, or I've snatched at the ball. I always used to tell myself 'this ball's coming to me' and had to clear my mind before the delivery.

A loss of concentration can be very serious in the first-class game. Take the Benson and Hedges Cup final in 1978, when we were striving for early wickets against Kent, after making a low score ourselves. Bob Woolmer was putting down roots and looking very secure when Eddie Barlow dropped him at slip off Mike Hendrick. We were obviously disappointed, but I failed to clear my head for the next delivery – it took the shoulder of Woolmer's bat, I hesitated for a split second, I didn't get fully across to it and the ball popped out after touching the ends of my fingers. Woolmer won the man-of-the-match award as Kent strolled to victory. That aberration of mine stemmed from a lack of concentration – and the cares of captaincy meant that such lapses would get more and more frequent.

Concentration is so vital for a keeper. I once dropped Roy Fredericks three times in an over off the inswing of Ian Buxton – two of them attempted drives, one a push forward. Each one went straight in and straight out. Perhaps over-confidence had something to do with it; I had just returned from Lord's, after representing MCC against the champion county, and I reckon I was feeling a shade complacent. Whatever the reason, it soon dawned on me that vigilance was an essential ingredient for a top wicketkeeper and I cannot see how he can combine his job with captaincy. I saw at close hand what it did to Wasim Bari. For a decade, he was one of the best keepers in the world, yet he was disappointing when I played two series against him, in 1977–78 and 1978. He didn't seem to be concentrating, he dropped a lot of deliveries and his generally listless air made it look as if he had the whole world on his shoulders. When the captaincy was taken away from him, he regained his form and kept for Pakistan for another five years.

Rod Marsh is an exception to my feelings about wicketkeeper-captains. With all due respect to certain people, Rod would have made a very good job of the Australian captaincy after the Packer affair. By that time, he was a mature, experienced player with a friendly yet competitive streak. He would have led from the front and his strong character would have helped ward off any doubts about his form. Many Aussie captains have paid tribute to Rod's tactical wisdom and I am surprised he was never given the chance. He was such a powerful, positive thinker that I don't believe his work behind the stumps would have suffered – but the Rod Marshes of this world are few and far between.

When I resigned the Derbyshire captaincy in 1976, I recommended Eddie Barlow to take over and I was delighted at the transformation he accomplished in the side. I had several chats with Eddie in the previous winter when visiting South Africa with the International Wanderers – he had already signed a three-year contract with us and I was impressed by his keenness and willingness to learn. At the age of 36 – a year older than me – he was full of youthful exuberance at the belated chance of extending his cricket education in the county championship. He struck me as a positive thinker who could make things happen and I was right. Eddie Barlow's captaincy at Derbyshire marked my happiest three seasons at the club; he made it a pleasure to come to work.

Eddie's first words as captain impressed us all. He called us together and said, 'You're to enjoy your cricket. I don't want any mention of the weather from any of you. You're paid to play for Derbyshire and I want you to get your minds attuned to just that when you drive here in the morning. When you're on this ground, you think and act positively.' He was absolutely right about the obsession of English pros with the weather. Time and again, we would sit in the dressing-room and I would hear an experienced player say, 'There's rain on the way – I hope it drops on us.' Too many seemed to resent going onto the pitch to carry on their profession, they loved a wet summer, where the card games flourished. I had never felt that way – cricket was too precious to me – but I was pleased that Eddie had spotted these negative vibes so quickly. His tactical grasp was also very good. He would take a chance on pursuit of victory and would not complain if we lost. His attitude was that the public should be entertained – a refreshing contrast to an experienced English pro who remembered grudge matches from previous seasons and would refuse to dangle the carrot because he had a long memory. It was all a novelty to Eddie and he insisted on taking the positive stance.

He really was a marvellous motivator. We were the first county to start the keep-fit craze that all of us now take for granted. Eddie left us a fitness programme for the winter at the end of each season and woe betide anyone who was not up to scratch when he returned from South Africa the following April. He led by example in that department: he may have looked a little chunky, but years of strict rugby training back home gave him the stamina to keep up with anyone and he was always as fit as the rest. Soon all the counties were following our lead as we went through our stretching exercises before start of play – and even when there was no cricket because of rain. Eddie ensured the cards were kept out of sight as we pounded round the boundary while the rain came down. Personally, I was delighted at his insistence on physical fitness; my friendship with Bernard Thomas was well-established by then and Bernard and I had often talked of the need for greater awareness of fitness by cricketers. It had long been an obsession with me and it was great to see the principles seeping into the county game. Our fielding improved drastically as a result.

For a man fairly long in the cricketing tooth, Eddie adapted very well to the actual playing demands of English cricket. He struggled a little with the bat on green wickets, but he showed enough class to underline what a fine player he had been. His medium-pace bowling was in the 'golden arm' category – a great partnership breaker, with a deceptive late swing, he could inspire us with a wicket or two. He was a lucky cricketer, but he made his own luck with his positive attitude. Unlike many South Africans I have played against, he was a very sporting player: no verbals, no complaints, and a refreshing willingness to see two sides of the argument. I know he upset some sensitive souls early on with his clipped, no-nonsense South African accent, but he certainly smartened up a few ideas in his time at Derby. Our chairman, George Hughes, was paying him a lot of money – double the rate of the ordinary capped player at Derby – but we didn't begrudge him a penny of it. He was tremendous on and off the field, throwing himself completely into the social side of life and speaking at countless dinners and fund-raising occasions.

Eddie had great experience as a captain in Currie Cup cricket and he quickly impressed; he was always trying something positive, imposing his will on the game. Even when the match looked like slipping away from us, he would come on and, like Ian Botham or Tony Greig, take a wicket with an outrageous piece of luck. I remember one John Player League game at Heanor which was illuminated by a devastating piece of batting by Mike Procter for Gloucestershire. He smashed 46 in eight overs and the game was effectively theirs. Eddie came on and bowled his fellow-South African with a perfectly straight ball that Procter just missed. We won the match by nine runs, due to Eddie's good fortune. To this day, I'm not sure whether it was a case of one Springbok being nice to another, but we'll let that pass. Eddie had a great 'golden arm' and never allowed a game to get stuck in a rut. Our performances picked up dramatically – the Benson and Hedges Cup final, seventh position in the championship table and big crowds flocking in for our limited-overs games. Eddie struck the right note when he said, 'the guys have stopped wondering how we lost and started to be angry if we don't win.' The likes of Geoff Miller and Mike Hendrick started to deliver the goods and it was a proud day for Derbyshire in 1978 when four of us took the field in a Test – Taylor, Miller, and Hendrick for England and John Wright for New Zealand. For years I had been telling our boys, 'We're as good as the rest, you know,' and now Eddie was helping to prove that. I had seen how players of great Test stature would shake with nerves before going out on a Test pitch but, once out there, they could deliver the goods. It was to Eddie's eternal credit that he made our players realise that a little nerves in the dressing-room meant you could give of your best when the heat was on, when you would have the adrenalin pumping.

When Eddie left us at the end of the 1978 season, we were all in his debt. The players now believed in themselves and were playing attractively. He also made sure we bought more wisely in the overseas market, although I still maintain we should have gone for a fast bowler. In the summer of 1977, Eddie arranged to have three South Africans playing for our Second XI – Allan Lamb, Peter Kirsten and Garth le Roux. Not surprisingly we won a lot of matches! In the end, we plumped for Kirsten, who proceeded to give us five years of batting brilliance that set him apart from most players in the country. Yet Peter never really came to terms with English cricket; he was always saying how tired he was of the daily grind, that he found it hard to motivate himself. That cut little ice with some of us who had been doing the same for more than a decade!

Although Peter kept going on about fatigue, he wanted to captain the side as well – that would never have worked because his moaning would have dragged down the other players. When he did get the captaincy on occasions he proved to be over-cautious, a characteristic he showed when leading the Springboks in the series against the West Indian XI in 1982–83. In the end, the treadmill of county cricket got to Peter and he returned home, leaving memories of a rare batting talent but an unfulfilled human being. John Wright, the genial New Zealander, fitted in more easily, although he took some time to come to terms with a run of bad form. John allowed himself to get depressed at a string of low scores but, as he gained more experience of English conditions, he scored heavily and attractively and relaxed more as a person. He is now one of the best openers in the world and continues to give us grand service.

Despite the undoubted class of Kirsten and Wright, I still don't know why we didn't sign le Roux instead. He went to Sussex and bowled many sides out with his hostile pace bowling – just what every county needs to challenge for honours. Yet at Derby, we always seem to go for a batsman or a slow bowler from the overseas market, unlike Essex, Somerset, Nottinghamshire and Hampshire, who have all bought wisely and well. Our record isn't too impressive in that department. Our first overseas signing, Chris Wilkins, the South African, batted and fielded attractively for a couple of seasons, but then went home. Next we had the West Indian Lawrence Rowe – a lovely man, but a failure for us. Lawrence scored seven Test hundreds, yet didn't get one century for Derbyshire. The big problem for us was getting him on the field – a bad shoulder, sore ankle, migraine, hay fever, he had the lot. I'd like to have seen how he fared under Eddie Barlow, but he had left us by that time. After Rowe came Venkataraghavan, the Indian off-spinner. We got a couple of seasons out of him, but I fear his heart was never really in it. A very nice man, he got rather homesick and left after the 1975 season. I couldn't really understand what we were doing with an overseas off-spinner when we already had Geoff Miller coming along nicely. What we needed was a Garner, a Daniel, a Procter or a Marshall – the kind of strike bowler that other counties seem to pick up easily enough. We didn't get it right in my opinion until 1983, when we signed Michael Holding after my overtures to Geoff Lawson and Rodney Hogg had been politely turned down while I was touring Australia with the England team.

I pick Eddie Barlow as the best of our overseas signings – with due regard for the attractive runs compiled by John Wright and Peter Kirsten. Eddie's influence was always to the good at Derby and he made many of us better players. Three years after his departure, we won our first trophy since 1936 when we picked up the NatWest Bank Trophy at Lord's. The self-belief and courage we all showed that day stemmed in no small part from

58

the positive principles breathed into us by Eddie Barlow. His marvellous leadership also helped my form as wicketkeeper. When the England selectors started looking at me again, I could honestly claim to have lost none of my skills since my last tour in 1975. Eddie Barlow must get some of the credit for that happy state of affairs.

CHAPTER 6

A MAN CALLED PACKER

I suppose it's fair to say that a Sydney-based millionaire I have never met was responsible for R. W. Taylor becoming an authentic Test player. Without Kerry Packer's involvement in the affairs of world cricket, I would have been doomed to sympathetic condolences about the dominance of Alan Knott. As long as Knotty stayed in the England camp I didn't have a chance and by the spring of 1977 I was convinced that I was too old to challenge him seriously any more. The future seemed to lay in the hands of men like Roger Tolchard and David Bairstow.

All that changed during the events of May 1977 after Kerry Packer had announced his plans. He effectively bought up many of the world's best cricketers, making them unavailable for their countries for certain periods of the year. Eddie Barlow had hinted at something like this to me during the previous summer. 'There's a revolution in the game on the way,' he had said, but refused to elaborate. So now we knew – and, for South Africans like Eddie, it was manna from heaven to be back among the great players again in a competitive arena. As for myself, it gradually dawned on me that I might indirectly benefit from Packer's grandiose plans. Alan Knott had signed for him, and he and the others were soon banned from Test cricket because it clashed with World Series Cricket. So Knotty was out of the tour to Pakistan and New Zealand later that year; he couldn't be in two places at once. I wasn't surprised that Knott had opted out: he had always said he didn't like leaving his family for months on end, and a shorter tour to Australia for a lot more cash must have seemed irresistible. For Tony Greig – then the England captain – it was a golden opportunity to fulfil his ambition of becoming a cricket millionaire and, for senior players like John Snow and Dennis Amiss, it must have seemed like Christmas, with their England careers on the wane.

I was surprised that Derek Underwood and Bob Woolmer signed. Underwood, a great bowler, would be an automatic choice for England for years to come and he always seemed a true traditionalist, a supporter of old-fashioned standards. I am sure he regretted the move, but he would never admit it. Bob Woolmer might have become England captain if he had stayed within the Establishment fold – Kent was an ideal county, he had been to public school, he spoke fluently and intelligently and he was an England regular. I think it was ego that drove Bob to sign, even though he made his decision after Test fees had been greatly increased, to £1,000. The Derbyshire lads who played several winters with him in South Africa dubbed him 'Bobby England'; he liked being known as a Test player and the prospect of being named one of the 50 best cricketers in the world by Kerry Packer proved an attraction he couldn't resist. It may have occurred to him that the likes of Zaheer Abbas and Majid Khan might keep him out of the World XI, but it didn't stop him signing.

The motives of the England elite were at the time of no consequence to me. All I cared about was the chance to take over from Knotty for the winter tour. Sure enough, I became England's number one at the age of 36 and, despite my strictures on Kerry Packer and his act, I shall always be grateful to him for that. Over the next three winters, I was to have first-hand experience of the pluses and the minuses of Kerry Packer's organisation The first confrontation came in Pakistan in January 1978 when the Pakistanis tried to play Mushtaq, Zaheer and Imran, three Packer players who had been banned by their board from Test cricket. We were furious at such double-dealing. Packer's hand was clearly visible in all this – he had flown them as far as Singapore and then delivered the three of them to an official of Pakistan International Airlines. Clearly Packer wanted to embarrass the official brand of international cricket, to throw a spanner into the works and hope that Pakistan's fear of losing would lead to the inclusion of the World Series men. The outraged England team voted to go on strike on the eve of the Karachi Test if they were picked. Our captain, Mike Brearley, had read a statement to the media deploring the intervention by Packer and it wasn't until the evening before the first day's play that we received assurances that Mushtaq and his friends would not be picked. The Board of Control for Cricket in Pakistan climbed down and said they would not be selected because they had refused to make an unconditional apology for being unavailable for the whole series, due to World Series involvement. There is no doubt in my mind that we would have refused to play unless reason prevailed: Lord's would have chopped our hands off, but I would certainly take the same stance again.

What we were against was the feeling that the Packer players could have their cake and eat it. Greig, Knotty and the others knew that they had made themselves unavailable for certain Tests and they couldn't expect to come scuttling back when it suited them. The same applied to the Pakistanis in that series – it had to be one form of cricket or the other, they couldn't pick and choose. Of course, Kerry Packer would huff and puff about the Establishment discriminating against his players, but he missed the point: his players were refusing to play for the Establishment, and they couldn't just creep back in when it suited them. I don't believe Kerry Packer ever understood the nature of cricket administration or indeed the special traditions associated with the game. His strong point was that he capitalised on the fact that international cricketers were being taken a little for granted by the ruling bodies around the globe.

Much nonsense was written about the effect of Packer on long friendships among players, that player was set against player. There was some short-term bitterness – particularly at Warwickshire in 1978, where the case of Dennis Amiss seemed to polarise opinion – but in general the players from either side of the fence settled down. When we toured Australia in 1978–79, we were able to see the rival brand of cricket at first hand. I was impressed by the television camerawork, appalled at the ridiculous comments by the commentators – every boundary was hailed as the greatest shot one could wish to see – and amused by the amateurish interviews with the players. The idea of playing night cricket in fancy clothing didn't impress me, and there was no hiding the fact that the games were sparsely attended. As the same thing applied to our Test series – partly because we thrashed the Aussies – we didn't make too much capital out of that one. Our touring party remained pretty solidly behind the Establishment, but it didn't stop us meeting the Packer players warmly when our paths crossed several times at airports on that tour. By that time, I think we all agreed that everyone has freedom of choice but can't expect to serve two masters.

The following year, we were back again in Australia, thanks to World Series Cricket. As part of the peace plan, we had to return to play three Tests, plus a three-cornered limited-overs series, also involving West Indies. That meant donning the fancy gear and taking part in the 'Pyjama Game' at night under the floodlights. I must admit it was exhilarating to watch and good fun to play in, but a dreadfully tiring tour. The Aussies were narked because we refused to put up the Ashes for a mini-series of three Tests, but there was no real disharmony among the players. The wheel had come full circle for the Australian Cricket Board – in return for peace, they had to give WSC the television rights and the power to market the game in Australia. That ushered in the era of the Fast Buck, tasteless promotional work and a glut of one-day cricket. The tail was wagging the dog from then on and each Australian summer a band of international cricketers would zig-zag across the continent, dancing to the tune of Packer's advertising men. For example, on our 1982–83 tour, we went to Perth three times – a massive trek across the desert, a day's journey. The traditionalists had lost out, despite the peace treaty being signed in 1979.

Over the years, I haven't really changed my mind about Kerry Packer and his version of world cricket. As in every argument, there are two sides and I'll take the pluses first. Due to Packer, cricketers at long last received money that was commensurate with their talents. I was as lucky as anybody in this respect: 56 of my 57 Tests netted me between £1,000 and £1,500 a time. Before 1977, I had saved nothing at all from playing professional cricket since 1961. I am not bemoaning that fact, because I had loved my time in the game and had managed a reasonable standard of living for myself and my family – but no one can surely doubt that we could have been paid more for representing our country. The threat of WSC meant that Test fees went up from £250 to £1,000 and tour fees also soared – from £3,000 for the 1976–77 tour to £5,000 plus £100 for each previous tour for the following winter to Pakistan and New Zealand. A remarkable transformation and, to be honest, it was too big a leap and unfair to those who never quite made the international grade. Cornhill Insurance deserve much thanks for their generous sponsorship since Packer entered the fray, but I think they should have given £250 of our £1,000 Test fees to the counties. I believe £750 a Test was more than generous and I can understand why a capped player with no prospect of international recognition gets envious.

There is now a terrific gap in earnings between an established Test cricketer and the good, solid county pro. Take my team-mate Alan Hill, for instance. Now there is no greater trier than Alan, a man who has always been a great advert for the game, but because he plays full-time in the summer he cannot follow his teaching career and get a post in the winter. He has to rely on part-time work to support his wife and three small children and hope he will get a benefit from Derbyshire in a few year's time. That's not fair to a grand bloke. There is a very slender thread running between a Test player and a very good county professional: men like Trevor Jesty and Dipak Patel have been on the fringe for some time without ever quite getting there and, although the gap in talent isn't large, the difference in salary and perks is huge. No wonder there's little sympathy knocking around the county circuit for a regular Test player, especially when the elite start complaining about getting stale from too much Test cricket, and don't put the performances in for the county.

So the extra cash at last gives the ambitious player an incentive and security for his family. The money has also led to a greater competitiveness and helped sharpen up the fielding in recent years. The standard of fielding is 300 per cent better than in my early county days and I believe that contributes to the spectator's enjoyment of a day's play. Professional cricketers are now fully aware of the need to keep fit, and that can only be food for the game. Another plus from Packer – the television coverage has improved, with extra cameras and a new dimension to their use.

That's about all I can say in favour of WSC's influence. There is no doubt in my mind that the game is less enjoyable now, because of the many financial considerations. Packer woke up the administrators to the need to make money out of the game, to an awareness of sponsorship – but the goose is now killing the golden egg. It is human nature that more money in cricket means less sportsmanship, less concentration on the virtues of a game that I dearly love. I can live with a mundane England side, but not with the prospect of a civilised day out at the cricket being spoiled by a handful of moronic supporters and some badly-behaved players. I am not happy with the 'win at all costs' attitude that seems to be prevailing in professional cricket. Of course time distorts the mind, but I know from conversations with players of my era that the game is not as pleasant as it used to be. For that World Series Cricket bears a great deal of responsibility. It actively encouraged the histrionics on the field from the likes of Dennis Lillee; it made good television and it did the ratings no harm. Yet the antics of Lillee seep through to our game in this country. Look at Robin Jackman – a fine senior professional, an intelligent man who loved the game, yet he saw fit to indulge in theatricals on the field when he was bowling. All this pointing to the pavilion, threatening stares at the batsman and blatant intimidation of the umpire is so unnecessary, especially from a mature person like Robin. One of the best actions by Bob Willis as England captain was to chastise Robin publicly at Headingley in 1982, when Robin pointed to the pavilion after he had bowled Pakistan's Wasim Bari. Such a crackdown was long overdue, yet I now see it at county level and all the way down to the village green. Some say the antics of Lillee and others add colour to the game, and cite the way McEnroe gets the tennis crowds interested. My answer to that is that people would come and see McEnroe anyway, because he is an exciting enough player, the best in the world. The same applied to Lillee: the greatest bowler of my time, a fascinating spectacle, yet he felt he had to behave like a moron at times. Dennis used to say that he needed to be like that to function at his best – but that's his own psychological problem, not one that should affect the game of cricket. It was important to the Aussie image that Dennis should appear the male chauvinist pig, the hammer of the Poms, and the Packer media fostered that image with glee. Unfortunately he did it too well and bowlers all over the world who lack his talent now behave like Dennis Lillee. You should see them in schoolboy cricket in Australia, as I have done at Sydney and Brisbane. It's the worst I've seen anywhere – the air is blue with bad language, the cheating is on a massive scale and the threatening gestures are rife. It's only a matter of time before the atmosphere in state games over there gets even worse than it is now, and then the deterioration will spread to Tests.

Since World Series Cricket, cheating on the pitch has increased greatly. Nobody walks in Tests anymore, not even the English. We just felt that abroad we would get sawn off at the knees if we played it correctly, while the opposition were allowed to cheat because of poor umpiring. I am sorry to say that I have stood my ground three times in Tests over in Australia on my last two tours – each time for a catch behind by Rod Marsh. I would never do that in England, but abroad we used to get a bit of a siege mentality about the umpires. It's so different when you're in a dressing-room, thousands of miles away from home, sensing hostility from crowd and opposition. You find it very hard to play the game in the right manner when you know that the opposition will beat you by unfair means. We have had to adapt to the ways in which other countries interpret the rules and, as a result, I have seen England captains on tour criticise a batsman on our side for walking when he knew he was out.

It is different in England. The umpires are nearly all ex-players and I believe it is our responsibility to help them. When I first came into the game, in 1961, almost every player 'walked' if he knew he had hit the ball but now such players are rarities, usually to be found among the older breed. Perhaps the younger ones play too much cricket overseas in the winter, because they are definitely changing over to the category of 'non-walkers'. I was never told to 'walk' when a young pro, I just accepted it was the natural thing to – to make the umpire's job as easy as possible. Now I believe the younger pros are being told, 'Stay there: it could influence the match if you brazen it out.' An incident in my last season crystallised the changing philosophies. An opening batsman who has played for England stayed there, even though he knew he had hit the ball, because he wanted a hundred. He was on 98 when Geoff Miller had him blatantly caught off the face of the bat, close in on the off side. Geoff couldn't believe it when the umpire said 'not out' and nor could I. A few overs later, he got to his hundred, turned to me and said, 'I'd have walked if I'd been on sixty, but not 98.' The sad thing about that conversation is that I don't believe he would walk at any stage of his innings. These days, that seems to be the prevalent attitude – you're a softie if you 'walk'.

Cheating proliferates in all areas of play nowadays. The appeals from bowlers seem to get more ridiculous as well as the dumb insolence shown to the umpire when they are turned down. Fielders shout 'catch it!' every time the ball lobs up off the pad and too often the umpire gets worn down by the persistence of the appeals and makes mistakes. To my mind, it is no coincidence that the standard of umpiring in Tests in this country has deteriorated over the last few years: men like Dickie Bird, Barry Meyer and David Evans are still the best, but their human fallibilities are being exposed by ruthless gamesmanship. There are now so many appeals flying around that it's only natural that the best of umpires occasionally make a mistake. My county and England team-mates often chided me for my hesitation in appealing but, as far as I was concerned, I only appealed if I was dead certain that the batsman was out. I was invariably obscured by the batsman for possible bat-pad catches, so there was no point in my appealing. At Sydney in 1979, the former Australian spinner Bill O'Reilly cast a slur on my sportsmanship when I caught Andrew Hilditch, without realising that I had not appealed. I dived forward for the snick and, at the point of catching, I closed my eyes instinctively. Everyone else appealed except me and he was given out. I had no idea whether the ball had carried to me or not, and that night the television action replays showed that it had bounced before I caught it. That was the first time I knew that it wasn't a fair dismissal but it was unfair to blame me. The slip fielders had a far better view of it because their eyes were open.

On just one occasion in Tests have I appealed successfully for a catch when I knew it wasn't out. At Brisbane in 1982, David Hookes played and missed at Geoff Miller by a good couple of inches – unfortunately for him there was a loud snick because he hit one of the rock-hard pieces of soil by the bowler's foothold. I couldn't stop myself appealing, I was reacting to the sound. It all happened so instantly that my reactions triumphed over my common sense. That was the only time I have transgressed and I knew that, if I had called Hookes back, I would have been blackballed by my team-mates: already in that series, there had been some poor umpiring decisions and the bulk of our lads were very much in the 'swings and roundabouts' camp when it came to mistakes by umpires. A sad fact of current Test life.

The Packer Revolution gave respectability to this element of mental ruthlessness in cricket, it also encouraged a hard, relentless approach to bowling. World Series Cricket also set back the cause of the slow bowler by several decades, I'm afraid. Its brand of instant cricket involved blood on the pitch, cracked skulls, the bowler exchanging insults with the hapless, ducking, batsmen and the crowd chanting 'Kill! Kill! Kill!' as Lillee and the rest came into bowl. I had seen enough of that crowd hysteria to last me a lifetime on the 1974–75 tour to Australia, but it got even worse in World Series Cricket. Its supporters didn't want the charm of cricket, the slow bowler spinning the web to a good batsman on a perfect pitch: they wanted heads split open, helmets and bouncers. Can you imagine Derek Underwood snarling away at a batsman? I can't believe Derek liked Packer's brand of cricket but, like all the other Englishmen who signed, he would never admit it. It was always 'Kerry says this' and 'Kerry says that', like a speak-your-weight machine. Nothing

Kerry ever did was harming the game in their eyes. It was a shame that such a chivalrous, attractive cricketer as Richie Benaud was hired to jack up the hype and give his seal of approval to the fast bowling bonanza. Just imagine it – Richie Benaud would have been considered a luxury as a player for World Series Cricket!

As a result of World Series Cricket, West Indies proceeded to dominate the next decade by a diet of unrelenting pace that occasionally spilled over into intimidation. For all their fine batsmen and brilliant fielders, they don't play the game in the right way for me. There must be more to top-class cricket than 12 overs an hour and short-pitched fast bowling aimed at the head rather than the stumps. Before Packer there were fast bowlers aplenty who scared the life out of average batsmen like me – but at least they picked up many wickets by bowling at the stumps. After Packer, the normal method of dismissal seemed to be a last-second fending off by the batsman to a clutch of close fielders. The ball was pitched halfway down the wicket and the batsmen had to play almost everything off the back foot. When it looked as if the batsmen were getting on top, West Indies simply shuffled their fast bowling cards and whistled down another – or just slowed down the game to a funereal tempo. Driving off the front foot and the wiles of the slow bowler became almost extinct. The influence of WSC had shown West Indies a harsh and successful way to dominate world cricket and the game suffered. So did the art of wicketkeeping, because slow bowling was so scarce.

World Series Cricket also spawned the growth of so-called supporters who love to parade their ignorance at a cricket match. Crowds have become much more vocal and demonstrative in the last decade – some sections cheer when a batsman gets hit on the head and roar their approval as the bumpers fly. The new breed of spectator has seen the antics on television and comes along to the ground determined to see more of the same. On Sundays in particular, we are subjected to the moronic chanting beloved of soccer crowds and decent folk are being driven away by the kind of mindless exhibitionism that has dogged football. A small element among an English crowd like to see the nasty side of cricket, but I don't believe the majority want to see the game tarred with the same brush as football. The crowd invasions at Lord's on Cup final days and the jeering and whistling are backed up by a graceless attitude among the players. Surely if a player is good enough, he doesn't need to resort to the petty niggles, the overt gamesmanship that so many now seem to love?

Clearly World Series Cricket diluted the appeal of Tests for a couple of years. After that, the Packer players returned to play with just the same intensity as before, as we found out to our cost on the 1979–80 tour of Australia. On the face of it, Test cricket regained its strength, but I feel it has lost that precious element of novelty. The mystique has gone because we have to play so many Tests nowadays. Money is so plentiful that the threat of pirate tours is always there to lead a Test player astray; thus the authorities have to organise official tours that keep the top players fully occupied playing Test cricket. I never complained about the glut of Tests, because it was always stimulating to build on a Test career that didn't get started until I was 36, but I have seen many examples of boredom and staleness from others. I wonder if the game's followers are also a little bored with the elite now? After all, they seem to turn up in this country with great regularity – whether it's for a World Cup, a full tour, or a stint in county cricket. Those in the top bracket just have to keep going because the rewards are so good. Packer ushered in the era of the cricketing superstar, the box office idol who indulged in promotional work, advertising, books, even male modelling – as long as he could deliver the goods on the pitch. Men like Lillee, Imran Khan and Botham have made a great living out of the fringe benefits because of their supreme abilities – but at a cost. Where there is a stack of money available, human nature dictates that you grab at it, even when the ability that rocketed you to that eminence sometimes lets you down. WSC put us all on such a treadmill and it became a test of character to cope with it.

Packer's brash marketing strategy appealed to the 'ocker' cult over in Australia. For the West Indians, it was a chance to escape from the clutches of a lifestyle where for many a lack of money would be a problem. To the South Africans, it was a dream come true: seven years after their last Test they were back in some sort of semi-official fold, where they could test their competitive skills against some great players. For the Pakistanis, the chance to compete in such a setting must have seemed irresistible to players who often suffered from an inferiority complex, because there was such a fear of defeat in their Test displays. For the Englishmen, it simply meant a lot of cash and I don't necessarily blame them for that. They clearly had had their fill of Test cricket, an emotion I have never been able to comprehend. As an unashamed traditionalist, I was against the way Packer conducted the secret negotiations, at his cocky presumption that he could call the shots in world cricket. Some of the cobwebs at Lord's needed to be swept away, but the Establishment was nevertheless full of dedicated men who had the interests of the game at heart, *as viewed by an Englishman*. I make that distinction, because I feel that the English game has suffered more than anything because of WSC's influence. They simply did not understand what cricket meant in this country: it could not be marketed like a brand of hamburgers, it had evolved over centuries into a sport that embodied many solid, decent virtues. I am sorry to say that those virtues have been gradually eroded since 1977. Kerry Packer may have made many of us richer, but he made the game far poorer.

CHAPTER 7

NUMBER ONE
AT LAST

With the influence of Kerry Packer uppermost in many people's minds, I just went about my normal job as Derbyshire's wicket-keeper during the 1977 season, hoping privately that Alan Knott's ban from Test cricket would open the door for me. Sure enough, I was picked to go on the tour of Pakistan and New Zealand that winter. With 20-year-old Paul Downton the other keeper – this after just seven First XI games for Kent – it seemed as if the selectors saw me as the number one at last. I took Paul under my wing during that tour and we had many long chats together about technique and the unique atmosphere of an England tour. To his credit he never stopped trying to learn and he deserved to take over from me against the 1984 West Indians.

For the moment, Paul had to play second fiddle to me, as I had no intention of allowing my form to slip after waiting so long for the chance. Between December 1977 and February 1980, I enjoyed a golden period in a fine England team, playing 25 Tests, appearing in a World Cup final and breaking the world record for dismissals in a single Test. I missed out in only one Test – at the Oval against the Indians in 1979, when the selectors told me they wanted to have a look at David Bairstow, with the forthcoming Australian tour in mind. Knotty missed the whole of the 1978 season to concentrate on his sports business and half of 1979, when he was again available for England after the Packer peace – so at that time there was no threat from that quarter. It was a thrilling time for me – keeping in Tests to men like Gavaskar, Greg Chappell and Javed Miandad and battling away against the likes of Dennis Lillee, Bishan Bedi and Abdul Qadir. Mike Brearley's thoughtful captaincy was a delight to observe at close quarters and, during that period, the England team was the best in my Test experience. We won series against New Zealand (twice), Australia, Pakistan and India and, with luck, might have beaten West Indies in the World Cup final. We lost a mini-series 3-0 to the Australians, but that figure was as deceptive as our 5-1 triumph the winter before. Many made the point that we were successful during that period because the Packer exodus hit other countries harder. It's true that Pakistan missed their top batsmen and Imran Khan's allround skills, that the Australians missed Lillee, Marsh and the Chappell brothers but, after all, we lacked Greig, Underwood, Woolmer and Knott (as a batsman, I hasten to add!). We had world cricket's best allrounder in Ian Botham, a brilliant fielding side and a balanced bowling attack. Bob Willis, Mike Hendrick, Ian Botham and Chris Old have between them picked up 850 Test wickets in their careers and their varied talents all gelled together for a time under Brearley. The batting was another consideration, but at least the presence of young players like David Gower, Graham Gooch and Ian Botham meant we often played attractively, even though we could have done with another Boycott for solidity.

My first Test series in Pakistan contained some pretty dreary cricket. Minus their Packer players, Pakistan were determined to avoid defeat at all costs and did not do themselves justice. They had some fine young batsmen and, in Abdul Qadir, a leg-spinner who was to cause us many problems in more than one series. Yet a collective lack of confidence meant that they never capitalised on our batting weaknesses; they always ran out of time because they had taken so long to score their runs. The First Test at Lahore was a classic example. Mudassar took nine hours to score a hundred and they batted into the third day. As a result, the first two innings were not completed until after lunch on the final day! Stoppages for riots didn't help and, after the rest day, the increased military presence induced a strange, eerie atmosphere. In the circumstances I was pleased with my performances. Our manager Kenny Barrington had told me, 'just be yourself, Bob' and I must admit I felt less nervous on the eve of that Test than in subsequent home Tests, when I was vastly more experienced in international cricket. At this stage, it was still all an adventure I wanted to experience so much. It was a relief to get onto the pitch right away, to feel the ball smack into my gloves at the start of a series – I don't think the rest of our team were as pleased at losing the toss! That first innings was the longest in which I have ever had to keep wicket and, in the circumstances, letting through just one bye out of a total of 407 was pleasing. I was annoyed though at the bye: I had bruised a finger and didn't take a ball from Chris Old all that cleanly because I was favouring the finger. Early on, I decided to stand up to John Lever's left-arm fast-medium bowling and I enjoyed that immensely – especially as John didn't mind a keeper standing up to him for the first time in his career. It was partly practical – the wickets were so flat that the bounce was very low – and partly tactical, because Javed Miandad kept scuttling down the pitch. He was trying to scuff up the wicket with his spikes to help the spin of Abdul Qadir and I reckoned that my presence behind the stumps would alert him to the possibility of a stumping, and keep him in the crease. Eventually, I did the same to the bowling of Chris Old and relished the challenge.

It was very hard, demanding work during that interminable first innings but the press said some nice things – and, more importantly, so did my team-mates. Mike Brearley, Bob Willis and Geoff Boycott had seen enough of Alan Knott's brilliance over the years, so praise from them was particularly pleasing. My batting wasn't unsatisfactory, either. I joined Geoff Miller when we were 162 for six and in slight danger of following on. We had to bat for a long period against Abdul Qadir's wiles and the slow left-arm of Iqbal Qasim but we hung on and added 89 in three hours. I made just 32 but underlined my main batting value – staying there to support the senior partner. It was good to be there with my county colleague and galling to see Geoff Miller left stranded on 98 not out when our last man, Bob Willis, was given out, caught in the leg trap off Abdul Qadir. For the first time, I could see what the cynics in our dressing-room meant when they said you have to get 18 wickets, not ten, to bowl them out over there! That point was underlined in the Third Test at Karachi when I achieved one of the best stumpings of my career – except the square leg umpire wasn't looking at the time! Javed Miandad was again trying to get down the pitch to John Lever and, when he fired one down the leg side, I was on it like a flash and whipped off the bails. It was the kind of leg side stumping we dream of – the batsman unbalanced while playing the walking shot and left stranded a long way out. Yet the umpire said, 'very sorry, not out.' I couldn't believe it and Graham Roope and Bob Willis had to restrain me as I protested that the decision wasn't even marginal. I do regret my show of temper, but such a decision was incredible and confirmed yet again the problems we faced trying to win a Test in Pakistan. Six years later, on my last England tour over there, things hadn't improved.

There were too many distractions and too much negative play ever to allow a positive result in Pakistan. Things got to such a state that Geoff Boycott, our acting captain, persuaded Wasim Bari to come off the field an hour early on the last day of the final Test. There was no real provision for it in the playing regulations, yet the stalemate was so obvious that no one argued. The pitches were awful, the cricket turgid and the incidents off the field – with the Packer players coming back from Australia – were a good deal more animated than the actual play. Nevertheless I enjoyed my first series immensely. I kept wicket well on unfavourable surfaces and my batting stood up to the test. I settled at number seven – an early indication of England's fragile batting – and battled it out to get some useful scores.

After the riots, the noise and dust of Pakistan we found New Zealand a haven of peace. When our plane landed at Wellington, we all let out a mighty cheer! The atmosphere may have changed, but not the standard of umpiring. Off the very first ball in the First Test, John Wright, my county colleague, was caught by me off Bob Willis – a thick edge, taken just in front of first slip. Not out, said the umpire. Bob was so furious that he roared in and hurled down two bouncers that both rocketed over my head for four byes. In his first Test, John Wright made 55 – the second-highest score of the match – and although it took him all day he laid the foundations of New Zealand's 228, the highest total in the game. A gale-force wind blew straight down the pitch on the first day and as a result Bob Willis was frighteningly fast. At the other end, Chris Old was magnificent, bowling into the kind of wind that made you feel as if you were wearing a pair of leaded boots as you ran in. He bowled 30 overs to take six for 54 and it wasn't his fault that we lost our first Test against New Zealand after 48 years of competition. We relied too much on Geoff Boycott, who had taken over the captaincy after Mike Brearley had broken an arm in Pakistan. Our fourth-innings target was only 137 but when Boycott was bowled off his pads – uncharacteristically playing across the line – we crumpled to 64 all out. No excuses. The wicket was sporting, but nothing more than that. Richard Hadlee bowled superbly, we had one of those mad afternoons when people get themselves out (I was run out for nought when Stephen Boock hit the one stump he could see from square leg), and we collapsed. Revenge was swift at Christchurch and it was a significant Test: Ian Botham's first great allround performance. He scored a century, took eight wickets and two blinding slip catches as we won easily by 174 runs. I made my highest Test score up till then, adding 160 with Ian after we were 128 for five. Again I was run out: Ian pushed one straight to mid-wicket and called. There wasn't even half a run there, and I was out for 45. As I passed him, I told him to stay there and get a hundred. He did, and more than made up for his running be-tween the wickets, which has never really improved. Perhaps that's why he prefers to deal in boundaries!

With the final Test a dull draw on an excellent pitch, we headed for home, with one or two problems solved. We had stood up pretty well to the loss of the Packer players and had clearly unearthed a great player in Ian Botham. He was to enjoy some glittering days from then on for the next two years. Our fielding had been brilliant – with Edmonds, Randall, Lever and Roope outstanding – and the bowlers were impressive. The batting remained a problem that was partially solved by the advent of Gooch and Gower a few months later. As for myself, I was pleased with my first tour as number one. I had faced up to pitches of varying quality: very flat ones in Pakistan and uneven ones in New Zealand with erratic bounce. Standing up to Lever and Old took me back to my Minor Counties days when I did the same to the quicker bowlers. And it was nice to keep for so long to the spinners, Geoff Miller, Phil Edmonds and Geoff Cope. On all my England tours, that one remains my biggest allround test in terms of pitches and variety of bowling. With the bat, I had averaged 22 in the six Tests and showed what I could do if runs were coming smoothly enough at the other end. I had to learn to concentrate far harder than at Derbyshire and it was good for me. Undoubtedly I improved as a batsman after 1977, whatever the statistics might say. At number seven in the order, I was still placed a little too high, but I would continue to sell my wicket dearly, come what may.

Back home in 1978, everything seemed to go our way. We won five of the six Tests against Pakistan and New Zealand and the team spirit was fantastic. Gooch and Gower fitted in right away and they made us a more attractive batting side. Botham continued his dominant exploits and our varied bowling was simply too good for our opponents. We seemed to be on a high all that summer, expecting a wicket every ball. I remember the Lord's Test against Pakistan as an example. After a blank first day, we got quick runs from Botham, Gower, Roope and Gooch. We then bowled them out for 105 on the Saturday and made them follow on. That Saturday evening, we knew how important it was to get another quick breakthrough and sure enough it came in the first over – Sadiq edging Willis to be caught diving by me between first and second slip. Sadiq was the man we wanted out because of his experience of English conditions and Bob bowled just the right line to get him to play at the new ball. I don't believe a full Pakistan side containing their Packer men would have fared all that better. Of course the damp conditions were against them, but our bowling was too experienced for them. We had outright pace from Willis, swing bowling of high class from Botham and Old, off-spin from Miller and slow left-arm from Edmonds. Three of those could bat, while Old could hit hard, given the right type of bowlers.

Our bowling was too much for the New Zealanders as well. Although they were beginning to blend into a good side, we never seemed to encounter those days when it all falls apart. On the occasions when we met some resistance, something happened to turn it our way. One instance of that: in the Oval Test, Bev Congdon was holding us up with some stern orthodox defence. Phil Edmonds started to day-dream while bowling and I spotted that he wasn't putting full concentration into his job. I mentioned this to Mike Brearley and he said something deliberately provocative to Phil to gee him up again. He proceeded to bowl one that pitched on leg and hit the off stump, an absolutely unplayable beauty. Bev said to me, 'You can't do much about them, can you?' and he was right. That was typical of the way Brearley and his team made things happen during that period. The only worry was Mike's continued bad form that summer – he averaged 13 against Pakistan and 24 against New Zealand – but we all felt he was a far better batsman than his critics believed. The fact that we were winning so well helped to deflect the criticisms of a captain who was a superb motivator in his own thoughtful way.

At the end of that summer, I was named Man of the Series against New Zealand by Jim Laker: a staggering decision in my opinion, considering that Ian Botham had taken 24 wickets in three Tests. Perhaps Jim remembered the days when he played against me in the North Staffordshire League, perhaps he was just being typically unorthodox, or maybe the former slow bowler appreciated a wicketkeeper better than most. I was very embarrassed and the newspapers picked up the point when they ran pictures of me mouthing the words 'Who, me?' when the announcement was made on the Lord's balcony. Looking back on that summer, I don't believe I have ever kept consistently better for England. I knew I had to concentrate particularly hard because the glare of publicity would be on me at last, having replaced Knotty for the first time at home. It is always more difficult to play a home series, as the team only meet up for six days at a time and you have to pick it all up again next time around. On tour, we are not subjected to the relentless glare of the British media and we can foster team spirit that much easier. I had 21 victims in the six Tests and cannot remember missing a thing. At the age of 37, I wanted more of this. Our bowling line-up was consistently interesting to keep wicket to and in the Lord's Test against New Zealand I stood behind the best selection of bowlers from my point of view. There was the pace of Willis, the nagging accuracy of Hendrick, the swing and occasional high pace of Botham, the slow left-arm of Edmonds and the off-spin of Emburey. All five were the best of their type among Englishmen in my time and together they made the most interesting line-up for me. It is staggering to realise that these five never again functioned for England as a unit – they came together just once, in August 1978.

If someone had told me at that time that I would still be keeping wicket for England five and a half years later, I wouldn't have believed him. To me, it was simply a case of doing my very best in every Test and hoping that the selectors kept faith with me when the inevitable peace plan with Packer left Alan Knott free to resume his England career if he so wished. Time was on Knotty's side – he was just 32 then – but not on mine. I managed to hold onto my form during the winter of 1978–79, when we went to Australia and crushed them 5-1. For those of us who had been there four years earlier for that 4-1 humiliation, this was lovely revenge. The Aussies contented themselves with the statement that we were playing their reserves because of Packer and that the winning margin was a flattering one. Both views are correct up to a point. We won so handsomely because we were better led, we had the kind of team spirit that stems from a winning run, we didn't rely on just one bowler as they did with Rodney Hogg and, fundamentally, we managed to climb out of some desperate holes when we were really up against it. Time after time, someone made a crucial contribution when it was most needed – the sign of a good team. Graham Yallop wasn't a dynamic Australian captain while Mike Brearley was thoroughly on top of his job. We managed our triumph without any kind of form from our best batsman, Geoff Boycott. The pressures of personal and cricket matters got to him on that tour, he became more remote than ever and I have never seen him bat worse. He simply didn't use his feet and Rodney Hogg used to nip the ball back between bat and pad. I think it was a tribute to our cohesive qualities that we managed to surmount Boycott's poor form and still come out on top. As for the Packer absentees, we knew that the Aussies would produce some good young replacements and they did. The likes of Hogg, Hughes, Yallop, Wood, Border and Yardley all advanced towards maturity in that series and have served their country well since. When the Packer players returned, they kept their places, so the opposition to us cannot have been all that bad.

The highlight for me from that tour was my 97 in the Adelaide Test. I got out just before lunch, following round a ball from Rodney Hogg that I could easily have glanced to fine leg. Instead I played it off the face of the bat right into the hands of the wicket-keeper, Kevin Wright. I've played that shot over and over again in my mind and I often wonder if I would have been given out if I hadn't walked immediately. It wasn't an easy one to pick up because I turned the bat on the ball as it went past me, so the umpire might have ruled in my favour. It was only on subsequent tours that I picked up the habit of staying there in Australia, so off I went. John Emburey, my batting partner, put his arm around me as we walked back to the pavilion – it was the last over before lunch – and all the lads were very upset on my behalf. Strangely enough, I wasn't too upset. I was more elated that I had helped put us into a winning position. Like all my best innings, this one had come when we were really up against it. When Geoff Miller and I came together, we were 132 for six in our second innings, a lead of just 137 on a perfect batting wicket. We hung on for hour after hour and added 135. Then John Emburey and I put on 69, so I was at the wicket to see 204 runs added. I wasn't particularly fluent – just six boundaries in six hours – but I reckoned that someone had to bat like Boycott with the great man out of sorts! I didn't get my hundred but that was one of those things. Strange that I equalled my best score of 97 – for the International Wanderers against a South African Invitation XI at Johannesburg in 1976 – and that I was out in the same way, caught behind the wicket. A keeper twice caught by the keeper for 97. In the end, we won the Adelaide Test by 205 runs, thanks again to our bowlers and brilliant fielding, but I was proud to have joined Geoff Miller in the crucial stand. Those traditional Derbyshire virtues of grit and common sense should never be underestimated! Curious to relate, I missed out on the man-of-the-match award. Ian Botham got it for his 74 and five wickets in the match. As he said to me afterwards with a grin, 'That makes up for Laker's decision last summer!' Funny game, cricket.

After such a dominant series, we fancied ourselves to win the World Cup back in England in the summer of 1979. The Packer players were back in the ranks, but we felt that our allround bowling strength and fielding would get us close. So it proved, after narrow squeaks against Pakistan and New Zealand along the way. West Indies had all their big guns back but, when we had them 99 for four in front of a packed Lord's, we felt we were heading for victory. Unfortunately, the lack of a specialist fifth bowler cost us dear. Bob Willis had been injured in the semi-final and his replacement had to be made up of three bowlers who were far from reliable. Between them, Boycott, Gooch and Larkins went for 86 runs in the 12 overs that Willis would have bowled – and they didn't take a wicket. Willis was such a good, tight bowler in those circumstances that he wouldn't have gone for more than 40 in his stint, perhaps even less. So Viv Richards and Collis King took the initiative away from us and they got to 286 in their 60 overs. Even then, we might have won, because we made a great start in good batting conditions. Boycott and Brearley played just the right game early on, but they stayed too long. They put on 129, but left us needing 158 in just 22 overs, and we were always behind the clock after that. Boycott had taken 17 overs to reach double figures and with hard hitters like Gooch, Botham, Gower, Randall, Larkins and Edmonds still to come in that was far too slow. With Chris Old at nine and myself at ten, that was a very strong batting line-up but unfortunately the big guns didn't get a chance to blaze away. Boycott and Brearley were too similar in styles to open the innings in a World Cup final and they played too well within their limitations. We needed that kind of graft in a Test match, not in a 60-overs game. In the end Joel Garner's fearsome yorkers in the gathering gloom were too much for us and we were left to reflect on a combination of bad luck and misguided batting. No one can legislate for the genius of Richards or the fearsome hitting of King, but that defeat was avoidable.

We took our frustrations out on the Indians later that summer, hammering them at Edgbaston and having the better of two draws before they nearly beat us at the Oval. I missed the Oval Test; Mike Brearley had been kind enough to ring me to explain that it was important to assess David Bairstow. I appreciated his gesture, although I wanted to play in every game for England. Now I could understand how Alan Knott felt when he lost his place for one Test to me in 1971, albeit for different reasons. I wasn't quite at my best in that series – I remember missing Viswanath at Edgbaston when, standing up to Edmonds, the snick hit me on the chest. At Lord's, Ian Botham made history by reaching 100 Test wickets in record time, but the brilliant catch by Mike Brearley which secured the historic wicket should have been taken by me. Sunil Gavaskar snicked an outswinger and it came to me at a very fast pace. It was too quick for me but luckily Mike caught it low in his left hand when it seemed to have passed him. I was positioned far too near Mike and I must have obscured him. In fact, I did most things wrong for that delivery – misjudged the pace, stood too near to first slip and fell down on the golden rule that a catch to first slip's left hand should really be the keeper's. Perhaps I was simply off form, some sort of reaction to the Australian tour. I wasn't at my best in the World Cup either. In the very tense game against Pakistan, I dropped Majid Khan off Mike Hendrick when he top-edged a hook and I tried to take it close against my chest, instead of baseball fashion. Luckily Majid managed only seven but in a low-scoring match that might have been crucial. I also missed two stumpings within a few minutes of each other in the World Cup game against the Australians at Lord's. No reason why – just an off day. There was some press comment that I was feeling my age but that was nonsense. That 1979 summer proved to be my most mundane as an England wicketkeeper and I was glad to come out of a mediocre period by extra concentration and hard work.

I kept as well as ever on the next England tour – to Australia – and then broke the world record for dismissals in the Jubilee Test in Bombay. Although that Australian tour was foisted on us by Packer, I really enjoyed it. Obviously the Aussies were after revenge following the traumas of the previous year, but that didn't bother us. It was good to play against their best team again, it felt like authentic Test cricket. Dennis Lillee had extended his repertoire of ridiculous behaviour – witness the aluminium bat incident at Perth – but he remained a great bowler. His performance at Melbourne was superb: he took 11 wickets on a very flat pitch and we lost a game that we ought to have drawn with more resolute batting. I was one of the biggest culprits: I had hung around for 90 minutes, keeping Ian Botham company, when I decided, for once in my life, to play the hook shot. It went straight up in the air and I was furious at myself. Overall, I felt I batted well that series: double figures five times out of six against some very fine bowling. Apart from that bad shot at Melbourne, I sold my wicket dearly, an attribute that many of our batsmen lacked. Only Brearley and Boycott grafted consistently – Boycott was unrecognisable from the forlorn figure of a year ago, while Brearley ignored the extreme rudeness of many Australian spectators to bat very well indeed. With greater application from the others, we wouldn't have lost by 3-0, a margin as deceptive as the 5-1 figure against Yallop's team. The umpiring decisions seemed to go against us just at the crucial moment, particularly at Sydney. In the final innings they needed 216 to win on a damp pitch that was right up Derek Underwood's street. He bowled superbly and soon after Greg Chappell came in I caught him off Botham from a very thick edge. He was given not out – that would have made it 100 for four, with just Border and Marsh to come. They ended up winners by six wickets, Chappell 98 not out.

At least Greg Chappell provided me with two highspots in that short series. At Perth, I stumped him off Derek Underwood in the first over of the fourth day; that pleased me in particular because I was clearly keyed up, ready for anything after a rest day. Often, one could find it difficult to get fired up so quickly after a day off. Then at Sydney, I managed the rare feat of taking a catch and a stumping at the same time. The ball from Underwood turned and bounced, it took the top of the bat and I caught it above shoulder height. I noticed Chappell's toe was on the line, so I completed the stumping as well. Officially he was out 'caught' because I had completed that mode of dismissal first, but it was a doubly satisfying moment.

I was very happy with my form as we journeyed to Bombay to play India in the Jubilee Test. Cathy was there to meet me and again she brought me luck (she saw my 97 at Adelaide a year earlier). I took ten catches in the game to set up a new world record and my pride at such an achievement was balanced by a sheepish awareness that it all seemed very easy. The wicket was surprisingly green and Ian Botham swung and seamed the ball all over the place. He was fast, accurate and resourceful and his competitive appetite was too much for an Indian side that was clearly jaded by playing too much cricket. The overcast sky on that first morning was ideal for Botham's swing bowling and we were helped by the fact that the Indian batsmen played in such a carnival way. They just didn't play it like a Test – Sunil Gavaskar, of all people, hit John Lever for a six very early on. They played a succession of poor shots and whenever they nicked one my way, I took it. The first catch was the most difficult: Gavaskar tried to pull Botham and it went miles up in the air in the region of gully. It was swirling around in the sky, but I concentrated hard and took it. After a time, I thought, 'It's going well today' and I finished that first innings with seven catches. The press boys told me that I had equalled Wasim Bari's Test record for an innings and that the best total for a complete Test was nine, by Australia's Gil Langley. I thought that sounded beatable, given the conditions, the quality of Botham's bowling and the weakness of the Indian batting, but I thought no more of it. You learn never to take things for granted in the game. Yet I picked up Gavaskar and Viswanath early on in their second innings and the record looked a distinct possibility. I had no extra incentive in my mind – you must always expect to get a dismissal at every delivery – but I must admit I started to think I had missed out as the wickets continued to fall without my assistance. Finally, I got the ninth to fall when Yadav edged Botham to be caught by me diving in front of first slip. I saw it all the way and managed to get both hands to it as it dipped in front of me. When we wrapped up the innings, Ian and I led the team off and it was a great moment for me.

We had already made our mark on the game with our batting, through a partnership of 171. We came together at 58 for five and my task was clear. Ian was already playing some magnificent shots and he continued to play one of his best innings for England – controlled, authoritative, with some textbook shots. Even his running between the wickets was almost faultless! He is such an easy man to partner in a long stand because there is never any pressure to take a chance to score runs. Even when playing within himself, Ian has such a great range of shots that he never seems to bat slowly. I ended up with 43 and Ian scored another hundred, but our stand was almost nipped in the bud by an incredible umpiring decision that, at the time, reflected badly on me. I hadn't been in long when I played forward to Kapil Dev and missed the ball by a good six inches. My bat contrived to hit my pad and that produced a noise that might have sounded like bat edging the ball. There was no appeal from behind the wicket, but Kapil Dev went up. I had my head down as he appealed – busy pulling my pad back round after whacking it with the bat. Suddenly I looked round and saw the slips coming towards me. 'What's going on,' I asked, and Kirmani, their keeper, said, 'You're out, Bob.' I was astonished but said, 'Oh! I'll go then.' Then their captain, Viswanath, came up and said, 'You stay there, Bob – I'll get the umpire to change his decision.' By now I was getting very embarrassed because I didn't want anyone to think I was protesting against what was admittedly a ridiculous decision, but Viswanath insisted I stood there while he talked to the umpire. Ian joined me in the middle of the pitch and said, 'What a carry on, eh?' and then I was told I was staying. I heard afterwards that much of the media comment suggested that I had made a fuss and that I protested at the decision, standing my ground. That is not true; I was simply disorientated and concentrating on sorting out my pad while the umpire put his finger up. I would never condone a batsman standing there, trying to get the umpire to change his mind. It was, in fact, Viswanath who prolonged the agony by telling me what he was going to do. It was a typically sporting action by him.

Unbelievably enough, the same umpire followed suit later in the Test. Geoff Boycott shaped to play Kapil Dev down the leg side and it was so wide that he almost toppled over in playing the shot. There was no appeal, yet the umpire raised his finger! Luckily no one took any notice of him and as everyone carried on with the game he slowly lowered his finger. At that moment, I realised what my incident must have looked like – there was Boycott, also adjusting his pad, head down, taking no notice of the umpire. Thankfully, the Indian side at that time contained some good sports, and it all passed off calmly enough.

At the end of the match – a comfortable victory for us by ten wickets – Ian Botham made a nice gesture. He had been voted Man of the Match, hardly surprising with his great hundred and 13 wickets. As we sat beside each other in the dressing-room (we always changed alongside each other because it seemed to bring us luck), Ian tossed me the match ball and said, 'There you are, Bob – there's the world record ball for you.' He knew it meant a lot to me and today it occupies pride of place in my drawing-room at home. Underneath all his extrovert banter, Ian Botham often did the right things, quietly and thoughtfully. Bombay 1980 was one of them.

After the rigours of Bombay, a fascinating holiday for Cathy and I. Accompanied by Bernard and Joan Thomas, we went to Kashmir, savouring the magnificent scenery and indulging in some skiing. Then to the Taj Mahal at Agra. As we toured this enchanting country, I savoured the chain of events that had taken me to places like the Taj Mahal from the cinders of Stoke City's car park. I was now a world record holder who had claimed 21 dismissals in my last four Tests, as well as nipping in with some sensible batting. Life could surely get no better for me. I did not realise that I was about to enter a Test limbo that was to last for nearly 18 months.

1980
A CRUEL YEAR

I came back refreshed from my Indian trip, convinced that the 1980 season would see me play against West Indies for the first time in a Test. They were the only country I had not played against, and I was looking forward to the challenge of watching their great batsmen at close quarters and trying to work out a successful batting method against their battery of fast bowlers. I was ill-prepared for the biggest disappointment I have ever experienced in my career.

The selection of David Bairstow ahead of me for the one-day internationals made sense. He had impressed as a batsman-wicketkeeper in the Benson and Hedges World Series Cup games in Australia a few months earlier, when I was rested to keep myself fresh for the Tests. David, a jaunty character with great determination, was a sound man to have around when quick, unorthodox runs were needed, some acrobatic work behind the stumps was desirable and there was hardly any spin bowling the ingredients for a keeper in one-day cricket. As far as I was concerned, David's selection did not threaten my place for the Test series. I was, after all, the man in possession; I had kept as well as ever in the previous months in Australia and India and was also gratified to have nipped in with the bat on several vital occasions. To my intense disappointment, Alan Knott was picked for the First Test at Trent Bridge. I learned of the decision by switching on the radio on the Sunday morning before the game. For the first time in my career, I had been confident of keeping my place – at least to start the series. I couldn't understand the logic of it all: why not pick Knotty ahead of Bairstow for the one-day internationals? If you are going to have Knotty back in contention, you pick him for all England games, because he was an even better improviser with the bat than Bairstow, quite apart from his superior wicketkeeping. Surely age wasn't a factor in my demise: Boycott was still in the side and, a year younger, I was just as dedicated towards maintaining form and fitness.

I received a letter from the chairman of selectors, Alec Bedser, the following day. He said many nice things to me, but it didn't ease the pain. I felt the selectors had gone back on their principles. I was not the one who had signed for Packer, who had decided he didn't want to play for England until it suited him again. I would have crawled on my hands and knees to play for England and had served a long apprenticeship under Knotty on three tours. Was this my reward for siding with the Establishment over Packer? By this time, the Packer players were all back in the Test fold and I must underline that I had no personal grievance against any of them – yet it seemed illogical that Knotty should be brought back when he had no intention of going on any more winter tours for England. On top of all that, I had broken the world record just four months earlier in England's last Test, as well as batting sensibly to help turn the game.

Ian Botham's accession to the captaincy in the summer of 1980 was probably the key to the decision. Mike Brearley had handed over the job because he would no longer tour and the selectors took the logical step of giving the job to someone who was an automatic choice and who would go on future winter tours. Such logic was painfully lacking in their choice of wicket-keeper. Now I had always known that Ian Botham rated Knotty's batting ability; his first Test in 1977 had coincided with Knotty's amazing hundred that pulled the Trent Bridge game round and galvanised Boycott into a century of his own. First impressions die hard – and, to be fair, Knotty often gave such marvellous displays with the bat, as well as keeping superbly. I am sure that Ian was worried about going one down early in the series when he was very much on trial as a captain. As a result, he went onto the defensive right away and opted for batting stability. Peter Willey at number seven and Alan Knott at number eight was immeasurably more reassuring than in the previous Test at Bombay, where I came in at number seven. It didn't work out that way – England narrowly lost the First Test and could never get back on level terms after that. Alan kept wicket as well as ever but had a nightmare run with the bat, averaging just five, with a top score of nine. Many of my friends and supporters gloated at Knotty's misfortune, but I would have none of that. I did not blame him for accepting the call, I was more concerned about the illogicality of the selectors. Knotty and I met up at Dartford later that summer for a county match: we had our usual friendly chat, he congratulated me on my world record and then confessed that he was astonished at his selection. He apologised, but I said there was no need.

Both Alec Bedser, the chairman, and Charlie Elliott told me that they had voted for me in the selection meeting, so I lost out on a three-two vote. It was no consolation. My only crumb of comfort was that at least I hadn't been dropped through a lapse in my standard of wicketkeeping, but because of the genius of Alan Knott. I am proud to say that in my England career, I was never told by selectors or captain that my wicketkeeping had deteriorated. So far in my 26 Tests, I had 85 victims to my credit and a batting average of 20, so I hadn't let my country down in my eyes. My mailbag that summer was predictably sympathetic – many asked who was the last sportsman to be dropped by his country after breaking a world record! I realised fairly early on that I would not be picked for the tour to West Indies, especially when Alan Knott made way for David Bairstow later in the series. The selectors were not going to swap one specialist keeper for another, preferring to stay with someone who could bat. So I missed the Centenary Test at Lord's against the Australians, an historic occasion I had earmarked several months earlier while on tour. My disappointment was doubled when I had to miss out on the various social functions during the Test because of county commitments.

I'm afraid I felt a little sorry for myself during the summer of 1980. Derbyshire didn't get the best out of me, because my head dropped a little. My tally of victims slumped to just 42 in 21 matches and it was hard to motivate myself in county cricket, with no international promotion on the horizon. At the age of 39, I was convinced that this was the end for me with England and I had to steel myself to knuckle down to the job at Derby. My team-mates and the supporters all thought I was as good as ever during that season, but I know I slackened off mentally. I had enjoyed a wonderful couple of years with England, travelling round the world and competing against great players in front of huge crowds – now it was back to a few hardy souls on a drab day at Derby, with the opposition batsmen blocking it out for a draw.

Thoughts of retirement flickered across my mind, but several factors banished such defeatism. Derbyshire were kind enough to announce that they had granted me a testimonial for the following year and I was deeply grateful for that – it helped snap me out of my depression and rekindled my enthusiasm for the game. I owed the club a great deal and would continue to repay that debt to the best of my ability. Professional pride stirred me into a concerted effort to overhaul J. T. Murray's world record tally of victims; it would help me concentrate on those inevitable afternoons when we fielded out to a dull conclusion. I calculated that I needed at least another three full county seasons to get there. Gradually, my self pity and frustration mellowed into a more philosophical frame of mind. Without Kerry Packer's intervention I might never have progressed past one England appearance in 1971. Truly, the Lord giveth and the Lord taketh away. By the time Alan Knott had tired of touring, I would have been too old; even in 1977, I was cutting it a bit fine to get selected as England's number one. Yet, since November 1977, I had been lucky enough to have my education enriched by travel, with someone else picking up the tab. During that period, I had been twice to Australia, to India, Pakistan and New Zealand and on a private tour to West Indies. All that had stemmed from the desire of a millionaire I had never met to gain exclusive control of cricket coverage in Australia for his television station. In his own way Kerry Packer had been my Santa Claus. My standard of living had been improved and at least I had played 26 times for my country without letting anyone down. Many contemporaries of mine in county cricket with great ability but less luck would have settled for that.

So life had to go on. Countless meetings of my testimonial committee and visits to various societies kept me busy during the winter of 1980–81. I spent my first Christmas at home for four years and my daughter, Claire, hugged me throughout Christmas Day in case I disappeared out of the door on yet another England trip! I even drove down to Lord's in January 1981 to wish the England lads good fortune for the West Indies tour (regrettably they had little enough of it over the next three tragic months). I managed to combine some testimonial business as well by getting a few bats signed by the squad, but it felt very strange not to be at the centre of the pre-tour ritual. I had become used to the annual process of trying on new kit, giving interviews to the media, and posing for photographs. Then it would be dinner, where the selectors and other dignitaries from Lord's would wish us all the best, a hurried phone call home and then an early morning rise to get to Heathrow Airport. I would miss all that – even though the pavilion doorman at Lord's still thought I was going and showered best wishes on me! I did my best to keep away from the press boys; I didn't want anyone getting the wrong idea, to imagine I was moping and couldn't keep away. There was time to have a cheery word with David Bairstow and Paul Downton, the two wicketkeepers picked for the trip – the union between keepers is very strong. I had a pleasant chat with the manager Kenny Barrington; within a few weeks he had died of a heart attack during the Barbados Test. I suppose I must have been the last man to get dear old Kenny's signature on a bat. I would miss him terribly. He had been a manager of some of my England tours and, along with everyone else, I learned so much from him. He had such a positive attitude, he believed in making every ounce of your ability count. Kenny had the gift of making people laugh and I don't believe he had an enemy in the world. Just once he gave us a glimpse of his batting class on tour. It was at Adelaide in 1978, on a green practice wicket. Bob Willis and the other pace bowlers ran in and tried their best, but they didn't beat Kenny once. He was nearly 50 at the time, and I must have been one of the few in that tour party who had previously witnessed his playing prowess at first hand. For the youngsters, it was an instructive lesson and, for the older ones like me, it just reaffirmed that if you have class as a cricketer, it never leaves you.

Kenny's death completed a sombre year for me, but it was all good character-building stuff. I still had my health and fitness, I knew I had lost nothing as a wicketkeeper and I had spent some precious months with my family. Whatever was in the minds of the selectors, I knew I had done nothing wrong, that I could be proud of my final England record. I had reckoned without another bout of selectorial whimsy. No less than 31 more Tests beckoned for R. W. Taylor.

1981
LIFE BEGINS AT 40

If anyone ever doubts that cricket is a bizarre, illogical game, they can consider the change in my fortunes a year after the unhappiness of 1980. I began the 1981 season determined to give Derbyshire full value and to stay in the game for at least two more seasons. Thoughts of an England recall were never in my mind – I had enjoyed my time among the elite, but now I owed it to my employers at Derby to give of my very best before the pipe and carpet slippers claimed much of my attention. I reached the grand old age of 40 that summer and my imperturbable temperament had to withstand many shocks to the nervous system, all of them extremely pleasant ones, I must add.

In the space of a few weeks, the following happened:

I scored my maiden first-class hundred after 20 years of trying.

I was recalled to the England side, and took part in two of the greatest finishes of recent years, at Headingley and Edgbaston.

I established a world record for number of catches.

I set a new Derbyshire record for tally of dismissals.

I played in a Derbyshire side that won its first trophy for 45 years when we won the NatWest Bank Trophy at Lord's.

On top of all that, I was awarded the MBE for services to cricket – spending a memorable day at Buckingham Palace – and my testimonial netted £54,000, a record for the county. Just to round off a memorable summer, I was picked to go on the England tour of India and Sri Lanka that winter – at last a full Indian tour as number one, after the disappointments of 1972 and 1976.

The first highlight was that maiden hundred. It was at Sheffield against Yorkshire, always a team I like to do well against. I think that stems from the early days of my career when Yorkshire had a good side, and their players never missed an opportunity to inform you of that fact. Well, this day at Abbeydale Park, the game was drifting to a draw and some of the front-rank Yorkshire bowlers were injured. The pitch was taking spin and perhaps Phil Carrick might have bowled better on it – but a hundred is still a hundred. The crucial run came as I pushed Carrick out on the off side and scampered a single, John Hampshire taking his time getting down to the ball. I often wonder if that was a rare piece of sentiment from a Yorkshireman! Soon afterwards, I was caught and bowled by Carrick for exactly 100 and started to worry. I had the awful feeling that perhaps the scoreboard was wrong, that I had only managed 99, so I went round to the scorers to check. I was safe, out came the champagne and at last I had reached the target. In terms of value to the side, it could not compare with my 97 at Adelaide, but I played more shots this time in admittedly more relaxed circumstances.

A fortnight later, I was back in the England team, to my immense surprise. Paul Downton was dropped after the Trent Bridge Test and the general feeling was that one missed chance cost him his place. Paul dropped Allan Border when he had scored ten; he went on to make 63, the highest score of the match, and the Aussies won a low-scoring game by four wickets. I felt that was harsh on Paul. After all, he had by all accounts done well in West Indies and also batted pluckily. The fact that he was dropped for just one error underlines the importance placed on the wicketkeeper: a bowler or batsman can get away with one or two mediocre performances, but not a keeper. I had watched the televised highlights of the Trent Bridge Test and spotted a strange technical lapse by Paul just before he dropped Border. Normally the keeper gets down into his usual crouching position as the bowler starts to run in, and gets up just after the ball is delivered – but Paul was getting down about two yards before the bowler delivered. As a result, he was too unbalanced from leaving it too late to be in a settled position. When Border snicked that chance, Paul wasn't in the right position to take the catch. I almost rang him up at the team's hotel in Nottingham to tell him what I had spotted, but I thought he might have wondered what I was playing at. I didn't want him to misconstrue my motives.

When I heard on the radio that I was back in the side, I felt initially elated for myself, then sorry for Paul Downton. The selectors just couldn't seem to make up their minds about the wicketkeeper: in just over a year, five of us had represented England. Amid such confusion, I rationalised the situation; I would, as usual, do my very best, expect the worst from the selectors and ensure it didn't affect my enjoyment of the game. I had reckoned without a strange feeling of tension that gripped me and affected me more than any other Test in my career. It suddenly dawned on me that a lot of pressure was on my shoulders – the press were glad to see me back, having pilloried poor Paul Downton, and the general feeling was that it would all be fine now that I was back in the side. Yet I had not played for England since February 1980; we were one down in the series, with a young captain, and I was back against the old enemy in a Lord's Test match. It was hardly the easiest re-introduction and I was undeniably nervous.

I was struck by the difference in atmosphere in the England dressing-room since I had last been there. With Ian Botham installed as captain, there was a slapdash air about the proceedings: players were wandering about and nobody seemed all that bothered about practising, even though we were one down against the Aussies. The lack of discipline contrasted with the air of purpose under Mike Brearley whenever we gathered for a Test. There was a lack of togetherness under Ian, he seemed pre-occupied with his own game and I feared the worst. He fielded at slip beside me throughout the match and again I was struck by the difference between Ian and Mike. Ian didn't communicate, he seemed withdrawn and the side didn't play positively under such a dynamic cricketer. He bowled poorly, bagged a pair and resigned the captaincy on the last day of the Test, as it fizzled out for a draw. I felt sorry for Ian; he was really down during that Test and it was undoubtedly affecting his game. I had always said that he was too great a player to be saddled with the captaincy and he never seemed to thrive on the job. It was the best thing for Ian and for England that he was replaced by Mike Brearley, and set up an enthralling Ashes series.

I had more reason than Ian Botham to be pleased with my performance at Lord's. Early in the Australian innings, I took a good catch to dismiss Graeme Wood – an inside edge off Willis that caused me to change direction and take low down – and after that I settled down. It may seem strange for a player of my experience to feel so nervous during that game, but I felt that the burden of expectation was heavy on me. 'Bob Taylor will at least catch them' was the comment I heard frequently at Lord's – which was a bit harsh on Paul Downton, and ignored the fact that wicketkeepers also have bouts of mediocrity. I just prayed that I would show my true form at Lord's, that the big crowd would inspire rather than inhibit me. So it proved and I was to stay in the side for two of the greatest games of my career.

The events of the Headingley Test have been catalogued many times since that great moment when Bob Willis ripped out Ray Bright's middle stump with a perfect yorker to give us an amazing victory by just 18 runs. One of the more bizarre sequels was that Dennis Lillee and Rodney Marsh picked up a fair sum of money after they backed England to win at odds of 500-1 against, with defeat staring us in the face. Well, I also saw those odds and missed out on £1,000 because I never refuse to sign autographs. Sounds ridiculous, but it's true. At lunchtime on the fourth day, we were really in trouble: five wickets down in the second innings and still 100 behind, with the weather fine. Ian Botham and Geoff Boycott were the not-out batsmen and after them it was the tail, with me at number eight. I went into the dining-room for lunch with Mike Gatting and Bernard Thomas and the Aussies were elated, cracking jokes and just raring to get at us again after lunch. I happened to look out at the new electronic scoreboard on the ground and saw the odds of 500-1 against England. I waited till the information flashed up again on the board, just in case I had imagined the figures. There it was again: Australia 4-1 on, the draw 5-2 and England 500-1 against. I said to Bernard Thomas, 'That's got to be worth a couple of quid in a two-horse race,' and nipped upstairs to the dressing-room to get some cash. I offered the information to the other England lads, but they were too disappointed with their efforts to bother. That didn't put me off, and I rushed downstairs to get the bet placed. As I walked out of the door, I ran into a swarm of children looking for autographs. There always seems to be more autograph-hunters at Headingley than at any other ground and I was besieged right away. As usual, I signed a few and yet the swarm of children began to increase. By this time, the resumption of play was just ten minutes away and I still had to get to the other side of the ground to place my bet at the Ladbrokes tent. Yet I couldn't get away from the kids and was conscious that, if I walked away, I would get the usual subtle Yorkshire reaction of 'Hey, bighead! David Bairstow always signs, you know!' They're not slow to get stuck into you up there if they suspect that one of their favourite sons has missed out because of you. I was next man in and had to be padded up as the players walked out, so I had to give up my attempt and sign the rest of the autographs. I thought no more of it until the following afternoon, when the last Australian pair were at the wicket. Then it hit me. The irony of it all was that those kids probably had my autograph many times over because I always sign for anyone who asks!

As for the match itself, it was a triumph for Ian Botham and Bob Willis, two men who had been written off by many. It was also a triumph for Mike Brearley, who came back to guide us through the tense moments and bring that crucial slice of luck that every successful side needs. As soon as he turned up on the eve of the Test, it was as if he'd never been away. He was cool, sensible, thoughtful and dominant in a low-key kind of a way. Without his captaincy on that amazing last day, I doubt if we would have won, despite Bob Willis's marvellous efforts. Mike was never flustered, even though we had no runs to play with. He attacked throughout and switched Bob Willis to the Kirkstall Lane end just at the right time. He must have been tempted to take Bob off, but he backed his judgement and gave him the chance to run downhill and tear into the batsmen. Suddenly, it all clicked for Bob – pace, bounce and line were all tremendous. At the end of each over, I would rush up to Bob and say, 'That's marvellous, it's all there – keep it going!' I doubt if he heard me, he was on another planet that day. Bob might well have been playing his last Test that afternoon: he had struggled with his knees and general mobility for a couple of years and in the first innings, although unlucky, he had figures of nought for 72. It all came right for him just when we needed it. We took some brilliant catches and took vital wickets at crucial times, for example when Chris Old bowled Allan Border with a beauty. They buckled under the pressure, because they knew they should have won. Even at 65 for one (the target was 130) I thought we could do it, such was the impact of Brearley's positive captaincy and the inspiration of Willis. Amid the frenzy of that last afternoon, I broke J. T. Murray's world record for catches when I dismissed Geoff Lawson. I knew nothing about it until the champagne corks were popping in the dressing-room. I only appreciated the achievement a few days later when the euphoria of Headingley had slightly worn off.

Of course, it was Ian Botham's innings that gave us hope. On Monday morning, I had checked out of the hotel, because it seemed obvious that the game would be over that day. There was no sense of defeatism, just an acknowledgement that, on this occasion, the Aussies had outbowled us and we were about to go two-down, no matter how hard we tried that day. Ian's cavalier knock meant we were only too pleased to check in again on the Monday night! It seems incredible even now what he accomplished by playing his natural game – when I was out, we were still 92 runs behind with just three wickets left. Graham Dilley came in and played just the right innings to support Ian. Both of them struck the ball cleanly to all parts of the ground and exposed the tactical weakness of Kim Hughes, the Australian captain. He kept Lawson, Lillee and Alderman on too long and should have given the spinner Ray Bright a longer spell. He was only given four overs and almost bowled Botham in his first over. The conditions warranted seam bowling, but Ian often gets himself out against the spinners and it does seem strange that all those overs were bowled by just three seamers out of a total of 356. Anyway, we didn't complain and, by the time Ian was in the eighties, we sensed it was going to be his day. He was slicing Lillee over the slips, mishooking into empty space and also playing some cracking shots off the tiring bowlers. Dilley, Old and Willis all kept him sensible company and, when the day ended, we were 124 ahead with one wicket left. We were absolutely delighted that the game would at least go into the final day, but it was far too soon to talk about victory.

I changed my mind when I went into their dressing room that night. I needed to get some bats signed by the players – the usual kind of request that every team complies with automatically. The air was thick with swearing and general abuse at life and I could sense a feeling of defeatism. One of their players took it out on me: '.... off with your .... bats,' I was told, and I reported back to the England lads that they seemed very down. Obviously they were disappointed that they hadn't wrapped the game up that day, that the bowling had been carved to pieces and that Ian Botham had been a little lucky. I felt that the psychological balance had tipped our way. Mike Brearley was the ideal man to exploit such an advantage and, the next day, they batted as if they expected to lose. It was an astonishing performance by both sides because the wicket may have been a little suspect but not that treacherous. The odd ball took off and Willis somehow found the right spots to bowl at, but they should never have been dismissed for 111 after being 56 for one; this after getting 401 in the first innings. Headingley 1981 remains a Test that Australia lost, rather than one England won.

A fortnight later and it was Houdini time again. They batted even worse than at Headingley, to fail by 29 runs on a flat Edgbaston wicket. Ian Botham was again the match-winner, taking five for 1 in a spell that destroyed the Aussies, though I will never know how they could crumble from 87 for 3 to 121 all out, with victory there for the taking. Ian Botham didn't even want to bowl as they crept nearer and nearer to the target. He felt that John Emburey's spin was our only chance on such a docile pitch. It took all of Brearley's persuasive authority to get him to bowl, telling him to keep it tight for Emburey to bowl them out at the other end. He certainly kept it tight – and took five wickets into the bargain. I never thought I would say this about an Australian side, but after Border and Yallop fell to Emburey they seemed to give up. Marsh, Lillee and Kent played rash shots and seemed to accept their fate. For a period afterwards, Kim Hughes walked around like a shell-shocked soldier and, not for the first time, I found myself wondering just how much respect he was given by the former Packer players who were still in that side. In any event, the contrast in leadership between Kim and Mike Brearley was striking and once again Mike tightened the screws in the last innings to leave them adrift. The atmosphere on that final day at Edgbaston was fantastic, reminiscent of the support the Aussies got back home when putting us through the mangle. Bob Willis was roared on by his home crowd and bowled very fast, while Ian Botham relished the big occasion once he came on and started to take wickets. He just brushed the batsmen aside by the force of his personality. The noise was so loud that I was worried that any snicks to me might not be given out by the umpires, and the whole carnival atmosphere was inspiring. We had just watched the wedding of Prince Charles and Lady Diana Spencer a few days earlier and there seemed an air of patriotism and celebration about at the time. Certainly I have never known such an excited, animated crowd in England as we had at Edgbaston. It was almost as if cricket had suddenly become the most important thing for most of the country.

That Edgbaston Test was more gripping throughout than the Headingley one, which really only fired into life over the last 24 hours. At Edgbaston, the ball was on top of the bat throughout and it was ironic that the much-maligned batting of Mike Brearley should yield the top score of the game: just 48. There

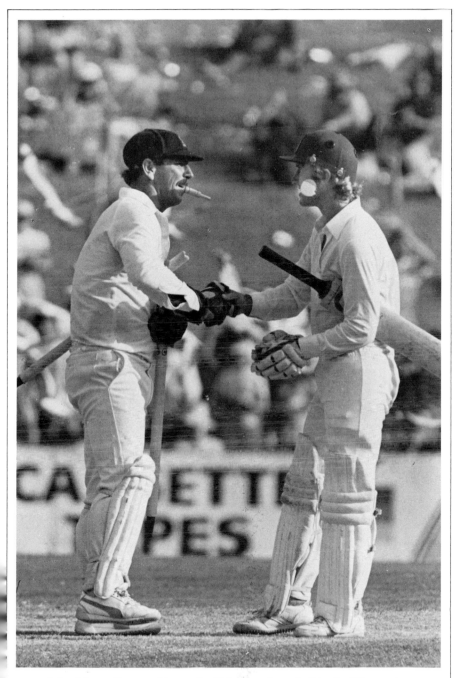

A fond farewell to my old mate Rod Marsh at the end of the final Test against Australia at Sydney in January 1983. We both realised it would be the last time we would face each other in an Ashes series and Rod was determined to grab a few souvenirs. *Patrick Eagar*

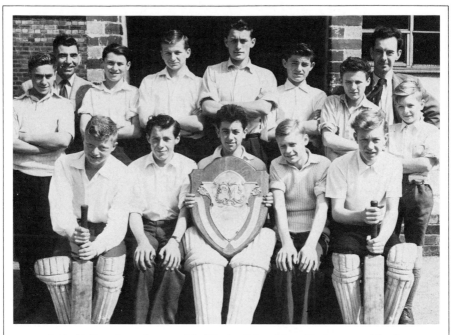

Stoke St Peter's — winners of the Hanley Schools knockout competition in 1956. No one could have asked for a better sports master than Stan Brassington (top right in picture), who was a guiding influence in my early days.

Behind the stumps for Derbyshire during 1963, my second full season in first-class cricket. The batsman is Middlesex's Peter Parfitt. *Sport & General*

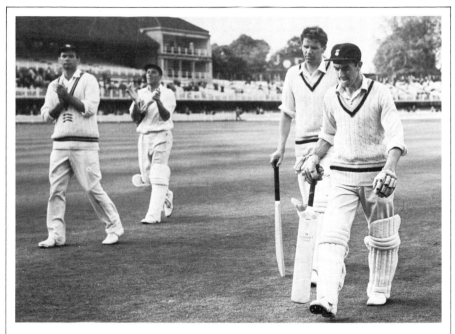

Derbyshire v Middlesex, Gillette Cup second round, May 1965. A moment to savour as I walk off the field at Lord's having scored 53 not out and won the man of the match award, though sadly not the match itself. *Sport & General*

The Derbyshire team during the year of the county's centenary. Left to right: Fred Swarbrook, Peter Gibbs, Alan Ward, Mike Hendrick, Edwin Smith, Ian Buxton, Mike Page, John Harvey, Chris Wilkins, myself, David Smith, Ian Hall.

Setting off for the 1970-71 tour of Australia and New Zealand in the company of Alan Knott and Ken Shuttleworth. Little did I realise then how long I would have to wait before being anything other than England's 'reserve' keeper.

Geoff Miller, myself and Mike Hendrick — Derbyshire's contribution to the 1977-78 tour of Pakistan and New Zealand, the tour which established me in the number-one spot for England. The three of us were also to tour Australia together in 1978-79 (where this photograph was taken) and 1979-80.
Gary Spark

Karachi, January 1978. Trying my hand with the most advanced system perfected by the Pakistanis for rolling their wickets into flat perfection. *Adrian Murrell/All-Sport*

England v Australia, Fifth Test, Adelaide, January 1979. Kevin Wright expects the worst as I manage to get a couple of runs to leg during my highest Test score. Wright had the last laugh, catching me off Rodney Hogg three runs short of my maiden century. *Adrian Murrell/All-Sport*

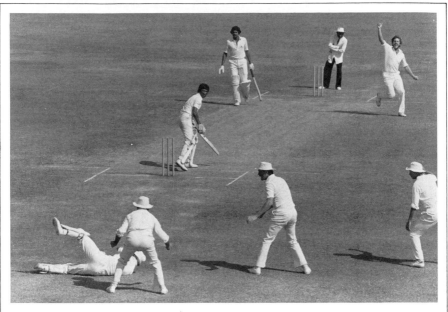

England v India, Jubilee Test, Bombay, February 1980. Shivlal Yadav ct Taylor b Botham — the catch that established a new world record for dismissals (ten) in a Test. *Patrick Eagar*

England v Australia, Third Test, Headingley, July 1981. Amid all the tension, I catch Australia's Geoff Lawson off Bob Willis on the final dramatic day to set up a new world record for catches in a first-class career. More importantly, we won the Test. *Patrick Eagar*

LEFT England v India, Third Test, Delhi, December 1981. Just to show that I didn't always gather the ball cleanly! Graham Gooch proved his ability to swing the ball late in flight, while I was left hoping it didn't go for four byes. *Adrian Murrell/All-Sport* RIGHT England v India, First Test, Lord's, June 1982. Malhotra ct Taylor b Willis — one of those chances that the wicketkeeper must take because he has dived across first slip. *Patrick Eagar.*

LEFT England v Pakistan, First Test, Edgbaston, July 1982. Pulling Abdul Qadir to the boundary during one of my best innings for England. My partner was Bob Willis, who finished 28 not out after I was out for 54. We added 79 for the last wicket and the following day we won a tense match by 113 runs. *Patrick Eagar* RIGHT England v Australia, Fourth Test, Melbourne, December 1982. The delight at taking a vital wicket knows no barrier of age. Norman Cowans has just had Greg Chappell caught at cover by Ian Gould and we are on our way to victory. Shortly after this great game, Norman calmly informed me that I was a year or so older than his mother! The younger generation have no sensitivity, do they? *Patrick Eagar*

England v Australia, Fourth Test, Melbourne, December 1982. Hughes ct Taylor b Miller. The situation was desperately tense when the ever-dangerous Hughes tried to 'lap' Miller — I changed direction and managed to hold on to the chance off his glove, giving me one of my most satisfying Test catches.
Patrick Eagar

England v Australia, Fifth Test, Sydney, January 1983. I mark my last appearance at my favourite Test ground by kissing the pitch. Rod Marsh is intent on his souvenirs while Geoff Lawson tolerates the indulgences of a sentimentalist. *Patrick Eagar*

were any amount of crucial phases in the game – the 24 precious runs that Willis and Old added for the last wicket in our first innings, the decision of Brearley to promote Old in the second innings, so he could slog successfully against the spin of Bright, and the perfect hook shot by Kim Hughes that went straight into John Emburey's hands at deep square-leg instead of going for six. There was the lbw decision against Graeme Wood late on the Saturday night, which gave us hope; we needed it with such a small total required on such a good pitch. John Emburey's tight, nagging off-spin in each innings tormented the Australians and his batting was invaluable too. John and I added 50 at a crucial phase in the game. I came in at number ten in the second innings with England just 98 ahead and two wickets to fall. I hung around while John swept Ray Bright successfully. Those eight runs I made may not have seemed all that impressive, but the runs we gathered together proved decisive. John's 37 not out was worth a century in many other contexts and, despite Ian Botham's efforts on the last day, I would have given John the man-of-the-match award. On the last day, he produced two unplayable deliveries to dismiss Yallop and Border – the best two players of spin bowling in their team – and his line and length were so perfect that the batsmen took a chance against Botham at the other end and perished accordingly. John took six wickets in the match, batted splendidly and took a very good catch to get Kim Hughes.

It was an incredibly tense Test throughout. The media pundits and the players were all caught out as the placid wicket, fast outfield and great heat failed to turn it into a batsman's match. From the first day, it was clear that runs had to be chiselled out, that good temperament was going to play an important role. More than once, tempers were lost out on the pitch. Dennis Lillee had a go at me for defending Graham Gooch's call of 'catch it!' as the ball rebounded from Lillee's pad. Lillee, sufficiently fired up by that incident, roared in and dismissed Mike Brearley for the second time in two days and celebrated by jumping over the stumps, clicking his heels. Rod Marsh had to tell Geoff Boycott in fairly blunt terms that he was out, caught at the wicket off Bright, as Boycott stood his ground. Bob Willis got embroiled in a rare show of petulance as Kim Hughes got under his skin with some mocking gestures. Willis followed through and bowled the most blatant no-ball I have ever seen from him, and then proceeded to bowl five bouncers in two overs. 'Dickie' Bird hopped around, clucking his disapproval and nerves got very strained on both sides. It was hard, compelling stuff, lacking the glamorous batting of Headingley, but an enthralling struggle that was won by the team which kept its nerve. It seemed remarkable to experience two Tests of this nature in succession and we all felt privileged and drained by the tension of the past fortnight. I was most impressed with the Aussies on the night that the Edgbaston Test finished. They all came to a dance in aid of Bob Willis's benefit and they stayed until the small hours, chatting pleasantly and signing autographs. It took a lot of character to come up smiling after two such disastrous defeats and it only served to underline the fact that relations between the two sides were as cordial as ever, despite any aggro on the pitch.

Although pleased with my batting, I was less than happy with my wicketkeeping. I felt there was something missing in my display and it was significant that when I caught Dennis Lillee on the final day it was at the second attempt – a top edge dipped and bounced out, before I grabbed it again. If I had been on top of my form, I would have got it first time. Although I didn't miss a catch and let just five byes through in the match, I felt below par. Perhaps I was being over-sensitive; after all, four of those byes came from John Emburey's 'swinger' ball that shot along the ground, giving me no chance, and, with the ball keeping low, I didn't let anything else get past me. For some reason, I dropped several balls that came through and my work in gathering throws wasn't quite as tidy as usual. I have always been a perfectionist so I am never slow to criticise myself, and Edgbaston 1981 goes down as one of the most mundane efforts from me for England. I had the feeling that I was going to be dropped, and so it proved. They brought back Alan Knott for the Old Trafford Test, no doubt to stiffen the batting that had looked so brittle throughout the summer. I could understand the reasoning: we were two-one up with two games to play and needed batting strength to retain the Ashes; but I was still disappointed. Once again, principles went out of the window as the man who would not tour again returned. Knotty did well, averaging 59 with the bat and taking some good catches. We won at Old Trafford and drew at the Oval, so the point was proved. Knotty put his gloves away until the following March, when money from South African Breweries tempted him to leave Kent for a month to play with Graham Gooch's team against the Springboks. Meanwhile, I was kept on ice for the tour to India, reassured that I hadn't been dropped for wicketkeeping reasons, despite my annoyance at my performance at Edgbaston.

I returned to full-time duties for Derbyshire for the rest of that summer, and concentrated all my efforts on trying to win the NatWest Bank Trophy. The sponsors must have been delighted with their first year after taking over from Gillette, because the two semi-finals and the final all went to the very last ball of the match before a winner emerged. In the quarter-final, we had a close call, defeating our neighbours Nottinghamshire by 23 runs, after getting only 164 in our innings. Then in the semi-final, we had an unbelievably exciting game against Essex. They made 149 in their 60 overs and we had to bat the following day, because of bad light and rain. The Essex seamers were as accurate as usual and they whittled away our batting. We came to the last over needing 11 to win. I was batting with young Paul Newman and Norbert Phillip was the bowler. Paul managed to hook the fifth ball to the boundary, something I wouldn't have been able to do, and we came to the last delivery needing one run to level the scores. As we had eight wickets down, we would win if the scores were level. All we needed was a single and I told Paul, 'run for anything.' Phillip bowled it just short of a length outside the off stump and Paul played it past Keith Fletcher at silly mid-off. We started to scamper down the pitch for that precious single but, if Phillip had kept his head, Paul would have been run out. Brian Hardie had scampered up to the bowler's end, waiting for a simple lob that would have seen Paul out by several yards. Instead of that, Phillip took a shy at the stumps from five yards away and missed. The ball sped past Hardie, the Essex lads slumped to the ground in despair and Paul and I ran off the pitch in a daze of delight. Amid the clamour of excitement in the dressing-room, I was told that my six victims in the Essex innings was a record for a 60-overs competition. Where would I be without those kind statisticians of the press?

I just couldn't see us losing to Northants in the final. Not only did we have a great record against them, but we were now on the crest of a wave, convinced we were going to win Derbyshire a trophy at last, after a gap of 45 years. Our new captain Barry Wood had taken over from Geoff Miller six weeks before and in that short period had inspired us. Geoff's form had suffered under the responsibility and he had also lost his England place. Barry Wood thrived on the challenge and got the best out of us that summer. He knew the game well enough, he was a great competitor with a marvellous one-day record and was a dynamic influence in the field. In subsequent seasons Barry got a little over-authoritative and went too far in dressing down some players. He wanted to be a one-man selection committee, feeling that as captain he was in the best position to judge the merits of players. I told him that he would leave himself wide open to criticism if he left certain players out without discussing it with one or two others on a selection committee, but he wouldn't have it. He should have shared the responsibility. When things started to go wrong the following year, he was isolated. Finally, Barry resigned the captaincy in May 1983 and left the game that season. I was sorry to see him go and still feel that he could do a good job for a county that had faith in his professionalism and the kind of fitness that would do credit to a man ten years his junior.

Barry Wood's problems at Derby were still to come as he led us to a tremendous last-ball win at Lord's. Northants themselves were no strangers to tight finishes – in the semi-final, they had beaten Lancashire by one wicket with one ball to spare, with Jim Griffiths, by common consent the worst batsman in county cricket, playing out deliveries from Michael Holding, Paul Allott and Bernard Reidy. If Northants could fashion a win out of such a situation, there would be no question marks about their temperament on final day. It was a marvellous advertisement for the limited-overs game, with 470 runs scored and the game settled off the final ball. We needed 32 off the last four overs with four wickets left and the light rapidly deteriorating. Geoff Miller now played one of his best innings, only 22 not out, but he was calm and resourceful, running like a stag for everything. The turning point came when he hit Sarfraz into the Tavern for six, then Colin Tunnicliffe smashed him for 11 in the penultimate over. We needed seven to win off the last over, or six if we lost only eight wickets: they had lost nine in scoring 235. I was next man in and definitely didn't fancy going out there in such an atmosphere. Geoff Cook seemed to take an age setting his field for the last ball before Jim bowled it. We needed one run to win. Colin Tunnicliffe swung at a ball pitched outside his leg stump, missed it completely as it struck his pad and ran to the bowler's end. Geoff Miller sprinted for the crease as Allan Lamb ran to pick up from mid-on. Miller got there just in time as the stumps were knocked down and the umpire said 'not out' in a flurry of dust and whirling arms. I felt so pleased for Geoff Miller as he stood there, arms aloft, unable to believe that we had done it. Geoff had done so much for the county, had been unfairly written off when he resigned the captaincy, yet bounced back to show his temperament was sound enough.

The emotion got to me straight away. I'm not ashamed to admit that I'm a sentimental man, and the lump in the throat was accompanied by tears – tears of pride that we had at last won something for our supporters, and tears of relief that we had done ourselves justice in a final at the third time of asking. No matter how many times you play for your country, it means so much to come back to your county and see them win something. I looked around our dressing-room and felt so pleased for some honest cricketers who would never know what it's like to go into the Cornhill Tent during a Test match – lads like Alan Hill, who had taken a great diving catch to dismiss the dangerous Richard Williams, and Colin Tunnicliffe, who had found his range against Sarfraz just in time. There was David Steele, my old mate from dancing days at the Stoke Palais; Kim Barnett, another Stafford-shire lad who in my opinion is destined to play for England. There was Mike Hendrick, friend and England colleague. A jumble of memories came whirling in on me as I sat taking it all in: what would the likes of Charlie Lee, George Dawkes and Les Jackson make of all this diving around and slogging at eight-thirty on a September evening?

When I settled down to play the game back over in my mind, I think there were distinct turning points. There was Geoff Miller's great catch on the mid-wicket boundary to get rid of Wayne Larkins when they were 99 without loss in quick time. The run out of Allan Lamb by Miller looked dubious, but television replays confirmed it was a good decision. Barry Wood's tigerish fielding and inspirational captaincy must be acknowledged, as well as the splendid partnership of 123 by John Wright and Peter Kirsten that set up the victory chase. Yet the one vital point was the field placing of Geoff Cook for that final ball: Geoff wasn't close enough to the batsmen on the leg side, he should have been right in on the edge of the bat, as Keith Fletcher had been in the semi-final. If Geoff had been closer, he would have taken the ball off Tunnicliffe's pad and broken the wicket with some ease. We already knew that we had to scamper a single somehow, so the initiative was surely with the fielding side. I wonder if Geoff Cook would set the same field again if he had the chance? Certainly none of *us* had any complaints!

That 1981 Derbyshire team was the best in all my years with the county. It was a far cry from the days when we had good bowlers and orthodox batsmen who could not score fast enough. Our fielding was brilliant – with the likes of Barnett, Kirsten, Hill and Wood outstanding; we had spin from Miller and Steele; an accurate bowler who was also a number four batsman in Wood; a good pair of opening bowlers in Hendrick and Newman and the left-arm seamers of Tunnicliffe to give variety. We were also well led by Wood and the batting had the class of Wright and Kirsten backed up by the allround efforts of Wood, Steele and Miller. It was a pleasure to be in that side and I am only sorry that it broke up almost immediately, with Steele returning to Northants, Kirsten to South Africa, Hendrick going to Nottinghamshire and Wood into oblivion.

So my season ended on a high, emotional note. I had played in four of the most memorable games of my career within the space of six weeks. At the age of 40, I still felt ready for the fray, those tight games had refreshed me. Here was further proof that the game of cricket would always make fools of the prophets and the players, that it was there to be enjoyed and not reduced to an exact science. I look back on the year of 1981 with great affection for all the intense pleasure it brought me. The splendid efforts of my testimonial committee brought me a gratifying reward, and that enabled me to look to the future with some degree of confidence. I was still an England player, despite being dropped again. J. T. Murray's record total was getting nearer and nearer, and I had won something with my county at last. No one could have prepared for the winter tour of India with more enthusiasm than me.

CHAPTER 10

LOSING ALL ROUND THE WORLD

After my fortieth birthday, I went on three England tours in a row and, although they all had their fascinations, they were disappointing from a cricketing point of view. Out of 18 Tests abroad in that period, we won just two of them – against the newcomers, Sri Lanka, and that astonishing match at Melbourne, where we squeezed home by just three runs. We lost four series, in India, Australia, New Zealand and Pakistan, and played under three captains in that time. It was hard coming to terms with our mediocrity but the fact had to be faced that, when my Test career ended in 1984, we had plunged down the world ratings. Undeniably it had become more difficult to win a series abroad – only West Indies seemed to have mastered that problem – but we were also hampered by the ban on several of our best players for their part in the South African excursion in 1982, and the fact that many of our younger element seemed to lack the necessary determination and character to succeed at the highest level.

After the euphoria of that 1981 summer, we plunged straight into gloom in India when we lost the First Test at Bombay through bad batting. We allowed ourselves to be distracted by poor umpiring and the vagaries of a pitch where the bounce was uneven; all out for 101, we lost by 138 runs. Our tour management made an official protest about the umpiring the day after the Test had ended and, although it was justified in terms of what had happened out on the pitch, it didn't really help our morale. The umpire we objected to (K. B. Ramaswamy) did not stand again in the series, but we still thought we came off worst in the close decisions. I suppose every touring side thinks that, yet we failed to lift our heads up and battle consistently to make things go our way. Having said that, we faced an almost insuperable task. After the horrors of Bombay, we knew that the

Indians would prepare slow, flat pitches that would need something fairly dramatic to produce a positive result. At Madras, the wicket was a batsman's paradise by the first afternoon and, in three of the remaining four Tests, the pitches were so dead that a first innings was still in progress on the final day. On the rare occasions when we had a chance of breaking through, the batting depth of India or the slow over-rate thwarted us. Add to all that, numerous stoppages for drinks, shadows on the pitch and crowd disturbances, plus playing time of just five and a half hours per day, and it was soon clear that we were up against it. We seemed to be in the field a hell of a lot throughout that interminable series, yet I didn't have a great deal to do, the ball rarely seemed to beat the bat. We were criticised for our slow over-rate, but that was due to the slow methods of the batsmen. Time after time, we were ready to bowl, but they would still be in the middle of the wicket, brushing away imaginary stones from the area, or having a tactical chat. We used to point out to the umpires that they had authority to get the batsmen ready to face us, but they never seemed to bother and they let them dawdle along. So we got the blame for bowling slowly, which was unfair because after Bombay we were well aware that the more deliveries we sent down the better chance we had of winning. Unfortunately, Sunil Gavaskar, a very shrewd captain, had worked that one out as well, and he made no effort to force the issue after the First Test. When we batted, they walked around as if tomorrow would do: Dilip Doshi, slow left-arm, would take five minutes to bowl an over!

I thought Keith Fletcher did a good job as Mike Brearley's successor to the England captaincy. In county cricket, he was always the nearest to Brearley as a tactician, although he was poor at team meetings. Keith was very good at discussing things individually on the field of play, but when it came to addressing the team on the eve of a Test, he lacked conviction and just contented himself with stating the obvious. After a time, one or two gave up listening because they knew what would be said. Apart from that, he did well in my opinion. He was popular and did his best at the official functions, even though he lacked the polish of Brearley. He wasn't helped by Geoffrey Boycott's attitude at team meetings; Boycs would sit on the floor, ostentatiously reading a paper while Keith went through his usual theme. He would pretend to read yet occasionally come up with a pertinent comment that showed he had listened to every word. I felt he might have given Keith more open support, but perhaps the prospect of becoming the top run-scorer of all time in Tests was his dominant concern on that tour. He beat Sir Garry Sobers' record at Delhi just before Christmas and only a fortnight later he was on his way home. Officially the reason for his early departure was 'physical and mental tiredness', yet the tour still had six weeks and three more Tests to run. Seven weeks after his early departure, Boycott was fresh enough to turn up in South Africa with the other English players who had taken the money offered by South African Breweries. I have no idea what led to the decision to send him home early. Some of my colleagues on that tour said he tried to get the non-playing members to come and play golf during the Calcutta Test, when Boycott was allegedly too unwell to field. I wouldn't know about that, because I was on the pitch at the time. Certainly he didn't look very well on the rest day of that Calcutta Test; he had a problem with his spleen years before, and as a result was never too keen to tour the Indian sub-continent. He made an exception for this tour and when he set up the new Test record he was very chirpy, loving all the attention from the media. Yet a few days later, he was apparently so ill that he had to go home. We all took his departure fairly philosophically: at that stage in the series, a typical Boycott innings was less vital than some cavalier batting from the likes of Gooch, Botham and Gower. In any event, he had never been thoroughly integrated into the tour party; you could rarely get through to Boycs unless he was feeling receptive. His early departure at least meant a chance in the Tests for Mike Gatting and Geoff Cook, who were superb team men throughout the tour.

Boycott's attitude wasn't the only thing to perturb Keith Fletcher on that tour. He also had to weigh up his response to the South African offer. As England captain, he was obviously in a position to capitalise commercially, but he took the side of the Establishment and refused the offer. I first heard about the proposed tour at Baroda, just a month after we had arrived in India. The five who eventually signed – Boycott, Gooch, Emburey, Lever and Underwood – were certain that they were going ahead, while they were trying to persuade Fletcher, Willis, Botham and Gower to join. We all discussed it quite openly in the team's rest room at various stages in the tour, but our manager, Raman Subba Row, never got wind of it. I was amazed that the press never got hold of the story, but the secret held. I was never asked to go, because it was clear that Alan Knott had been lined up to be the team's wicketkeeper. Bob Willis, Ian Botham and David Gower all said they were going to turn it down and the captain tried to talk the rest of them out of it. In August 1981, all county cricketers had received a letter from the Test and County Cricket Board, warning of the repercussions if they went as a team (not to coach or play individually) to South Africa. To me, the warning was pretty clear and Keith Fletcher let all of the lads realise the implications when we were in India. Graham Gooch and the others were wrong to say afterwards that they didn't realise the full implications of what they had done, because it was thrashed out often enough in our team room before any of them signed.

Graham and John Emburey, who were close friends, kept going on about the financial security that was beckoning and I suppose it must have seemed very tempting on a long, hard slog through India, when the cricket was boring. Yet both were such good players that they were sure to reap enough rewards over the next few years, playing for England at £1,500 a time. That was my opinion, but they were unsure about keeping their places. They had both been dropped the previous summer against the Australians, but that was due in my opinion to unfavourable wickets for Emburey's spin (apart from Edgbaston) and a short period of staleness from Gooch after the battering he had endured from West Indies over two Test series since June 1980. Both would surely come back, refreshed and ready to play for England for years. Yet John surprised me during the Sri Lankan Test, after the Indian leg of the tour. He had been a little down because he hadn't got many wickets in India and he needed to be coaxed into bowling at his best against Sri Lanka. At one stage, we were there for the taking; they were 140 for two, a lead of 135 and the ball was turning square. At tea on the third day, Bob Willis tore into us, saying he didn't fancy going home after losing the inaugural Test against the Sri Lankans and that we needed to pull our fingers out. I tried to get Emburey into the right frame of mind, saying, 'Come on, John, you bowl this lot out – the ball's turning square.' John didn't seem to fancy his chances, he thought the ball wasn't turning too much. I had to remind him of how well he had bowled at Edgbaston against the Australians – anything to snap him out of his negative mood. In the end, John took six for 33, we bowled them out for 175 and we won by seven wickets. It could have been a lot closer and that conversation was a graphic insight into the mind of an international sportsman who feels a little defeatist. When your mind is switched onto an insecure feeling, you can't really imagine you will be an England regular, and must be tempted by the lure of easy money. Cricketers aren't the best at thinking things through logically and calmly.

I knew the SAB players would get banned, but not for three years. I think they deserved a one-year ban, because they had been given their warning and chose to ignore it, but three years seemed excessive to me. The TCCB imposed the ban to preserve international multi-racial cricket, but they were clearly bowing to political pressures. They wanted to save the World Cup in 1983, and also the visit to England of West Indies the following year. I believe the TCCB should have called the bluff of the black member countries of the ICC. In voting terms, the white countries were now outnumbered four-three and it would seem that the black countries would always prevail in such circumstances. It was said that West Indies had refused to agree to a reduction of the ban, even though the ICC had just agreed that no country could tell another who should be in their team! So we had the situation where the black countries seemed to be telling us we had to do without Gooch and the rest for the full three years, even though I am sure most of the cricket governing bodies would have been perfectly happy at a reduction of the ban. Unfortunately the politicians had got involved in a big way and they had to have the final word. Mrs Ghandi had put her spoke in just before we left for India in October 1981 and no doubt she felt incensed at Geoff Boycott touring South Africa after he had issued a statement deploring apartheid in order to save the England tour. World cricket was now a political issue, as the Jackman affair in Guyana earlier in 1981 underlined. Yet if we had called their bluff, I am certain that West Indies would have come over to defend the World Cup and to try to thrash us in 1984. For a start, their players needed the money, otherwise they too would have gone to South Africa in droves. I reckon the politicians would have had to bend to the will of the people in West Indies, India, Pakistan and Sri Lanka if the cricket authorities had only realised the power of public opinion.

There is no doubt in my mind that England suffered greatly from the suspension of the 15 who had gone to South Africa, and all subsequent criticism of our performances should bear that factor in mind. About half at least of the 15 would have been

107

picked for England over the next year or so. Gooch and Emburey would have been certainties, Wayne Larkins and Peter Willey must have had a very good chance and, bearing in mind the selectors' attitude in previous seasons, Alan Knott would have been in contention. Derek Underwood could never be ruled out and, in terms of class, Dennis Amiss has always impressed me, even though a little long in the tooth by 1982. I doubt if Geoff Boycott would have returned, nor Mike Hendrick, Chris Old or John Lever – but England would certainly have been a more powerful unit if they could have added these players to the likes of Botham, Gower and Willis over the next three years.

So the England captain faced a few problems when the English season began in 1982. I assumed Keith Fletcher would continue in the job, but they gave it to Bob Willis instead. I must admit it came as a shock: Fletch had done as well as possible in difficult circumstances in India and he had taken the side of the Establishment over the South Africa issue. Perhaps the manager's report was unfavourable, perhaps he got unfairly blamed for the slow over-rate – in any event, I feel he was hard done by. The appointment of Bob Willis came as big a surprise as the sacking of Fletch, but on balance it made sense. We needed a senior player in charge of a team that was in a state of flux. Bob was a strongminded person, who was very good indeed at putting his ideas across in team meetings. I didn't think that, at the age of 33, his form would be affected: intelligent and experienced, he knew the game well and seemed to know exactly what he could get out of himself as a fast bowler. Bob had worked out how to bowl and his only problem would be keeping fit; he was dedicated enough to do that, and so it proved. I felt there was no case for giving it to David Gower: he was too young and too important a batsman to run the risk of losing form through the cares of captaincy. The same applied to Botham. Bob had been around on the England scene since 1970 and he would be trying his utmost. I think he did as well as anyone could expect in his time as England captain. He did very well in his first summer – against India and Pakistan – but then the opposition got harder and we were deservedly beaten in Australia. He didn't get any worse as captain and, unlike previous incumbents, his form held up. He was still our best, most consistent bowler up to the end of his England career.

Much has been made of the fact that the team under Bob seemed to go in for 'captaincy by committee', with people like

Botham, Gower and myself directing operations while Bob looked on. That may have looked the case, but Bob was always in charge. Right from the start, he told us that he wanted suggestions from everyone because he was bound to miss a few things when bowling flat out. He expected us to chip in and I think it was done diplomatically enough. We channelled a lot of thoughts through David Gower and he would have a word as Bob followed through after bowling. The media had got used to the figure of Mike Brearley at slip, calmly directing operations, but it could never be the same with Bob. It's a pity that his knees couldn't allow him to bend down at slip, because he was a very good catcher and would have been more obviously in charge as captain from such a position. When the cameras used to pick out Bob at mid-on it may have looked as if he had switched off: he would have his arms folded, or his chin resting on his hand; but he wasn't day-dreaming. Bob was a very deep thinker about the game and he worried a lot when he was captain. An undemonstrative man, it just wasn't his style to rush around clapping his hands like a Tony Greig; he was more of a man who would comment out of the corner of his mouth, but invariably he was very sound in his observations. Of course, Bob made mistakes as captain. He had a bee in his bonnet about Phil Edmonds and ought to have taken him on his three tours as captain. The selection of three off-spinners for the 1982–83 Australian tour struck me as very strange, although I'm not sure that Bob was fully in agreement with that one. Bob also allowed Ian Botham too long a rein from 1982 onwards, Ian had started to decline as a bowler, yet he still managed to talk himself on too often, and then he stayed on, although disappearing for four an over. The captain should have been harder with Ian for his own good, even though he has always been a lucky bowler.

For all that, I place more pluses than minuses against Bob Willis as England captain. He was loyal and respected by the players because he gave everything he had to the job of being fast bowler and captain. Although a caretaker captain because of age and knee worries, he threw himself into the job and did his best in a weak side. Tactically, he was no Brearley, but very few are. Apart from that, he lacked Brearley's wide choice of match-winning bowlers.

Both Bob and Peter May, the new chairman of selectors, placed great emphasis on good behaviour on the pitch and, from 1982 onwards, we saw a welcome improvement in that department from the England team. We were told not to hang around if given out, whatever the circumstances, and players like Robin Jackman and Phil Edmonds were given well-deserved rockets that summer for isolated instances of bad behaviour on the pitch. There were few problems with the genial India side, but things got a little inflammatory when the Pakistanis started to complain about our umpiring. I grant that our umpires were a little below par in the 1982 Tests but they weren't helped by ridiculous appeals from bowlers like Abdul Qadir, histrionic gestures when the appeal was turned down and continued complaints from the captain, Imran Khan. Anyone who has toured Pakistan is well aware of the standards of umpiring out there and it was nonsense to suggest that ours had fallen to that level. Bob Willis was right to decline to comment about the umpiring; we could have groused a little about some of the decisions, but we knew that it would be a waste of time and that our umpires were simply out of form, just like a player.

The tenseness of the Pakistan series only served to underline the umpiring lapses. Imran Khan was an inspirational captain and a marvellous allrounder and he integrated the Pakistanis into a team to respect. We managed to squeeze home at Headingley to win the series two-one, but it could have gone either way. I was happy with my performances on either side of the stumps; I got 54 at Edgbaston, 24 not out at Lord's that almost got us a draw, and I helped Vic Marks steer us home by three wickets at Headingley. Once again, I got some runs when they were most needed.

Imran Khan's magnificent bowling had exposed our weakness against the short-pitched delivery and unfortunately that lost us the Ashes when we toured Australia in 1982–83. At that time in English cricket, we had the one bouncer per over rule that became a little farcical in its interpretation. As a result, we struggled against Imran and, when we got to Australia, we were out of practice against the short stuff. The bouncer regulations didn't apply to Tests abroad and we looked unimpressive against Lawson, Thomson, Hogg and Rackemann. We needed consistent hostility at both ends, but young Norman Cowans was still learning his trade on that tour and Ian Botham was a big disappointment with the ball. It might have been so different if Dennis Lillee hadn't broken down with knee trouble and Terry Alderman dislocated his shoulder at Perth in the First Test. Both these bowlers relied predominantly on pitching the ball up to make it swing and, despite Lillee's greatness, we looked reasonably happy against them at Perth. Then Alderman stupidly chased a drunken spectator and put himself out for the rest of the season, while Lillee bowed to the passage of time. That let in Thommo and the rest and they had no qualms about bouncing us. The front-foot techniques of two of our openers, Chris Tavaré and Geoff Cook, left them ill at ease against the short-pitched delivery and we never really managed to get a start. Geoff Lawson was the best fast bowler in the series, while you never knew what to expect from Thommo. Rodney Hogg had one or two things to prove after his disappointments in England in 1981 and he bowled very well indeed. It must be said that the umpires were a little lax in permitting so much intimidatory bowling but we never really shaped up against it, particularly at Brisbane, where Thommo was warned for intimidation.

By the time we got to Adelaide for the Third Test, our batsmen were generally out of form and lacking confidence. The fast, short-pitched stuff had come as a shock to the system, especially as we lacked the firepower to answer back. It was the lack of batting confidence that lost us a Test we should have saved. We looked at the Adelaide wicket the day before the match and it looked a typical belter. From my previous experience of Australian tours, Adelaide rewards the pace bowlers in the first session and, after that, it rolls out a beauty. If Chris Tavaré could occupy one end for a time we would be safe. When asked for my opinion, I said, 'bat if we win the toss', but the batsmen would have none of it. Bob won the toss, and against his better judgement, opted to protect his batsmen and fielded first. Of course we tried our best but they knocked up 438 on a docile pitch. Our batsmen, reprieved for a time, still played poorly against Lawson, Hogg and Thomson, who took 17 wickets in the match, and we lost by eight wickets.

That was very much an avoidable defeat and it stemmed from negative thinking. Our batsmen were out of form and our bowling was proving to be weak: at Adelaide, first change for us on a perfect wicket was Derek Pringle, fresh out of Cambridge! Our catching may have been good, but some of our fielding was poor, with certain players not applying themselves. I shudder at the thought of one incident in the Perth Test: the first ball of the day was turned down to fine leg off Bob Willis to Derek Pringle, who had contrived to be looking elsewhere. Bob was screaming at the top of his voice to Derek, who woke up in time to give chase to a

111

ball that had gone past him. That was a far cry from the days when we had John Lever out in the deep for England. Derek Pringle was an enigma on that tour. At times he batted and bowled well, but he never put it all together. He would run in and bounce us in the nets, but fail to deliver the goods out in the middle. We would say, 'It's no good hitting us in the ribs, do it to them,' but it was fruitless.

We came to Melbourne two-down in the series, feeling very low, conscious that we should have blocked it out for a draw at Adelaide. Our batsmen seemed to lack character, they weren't going on to big hundreds after doing the difficult part of getting set. Worse still, their collective failings had influenced the tactics when we won the toss at Adelaide, and then they lost us the game when they should have done themselves justice. For a time, such criticism was muted as we took part in a fabulous Test at Melbourne. For sustained excitement over five days, I have never played in anything like it. They lead us by three runs on first innings, yet we finally triumphed by three runs to open up the series again.

The real drama happened on that last morning when Allan Border and Jeff Thomson got so near to the target of 292, but the previous day's play was almost unbearably tense. Norman Cowans came good at last after being carefully nursed by Bob Willis. On a wicket of uneven bounce, he bowled fast and straight, and we had them 218 for nine with an hour left on the fourth day. Things started to go wrong then, and we were criticised for our tactics. As soon as Thommo came in, he started slogging. Clearly he thought that was the only way to get near the target and at least he would go down bravely, with all guns blazing. I don't know how he managed to stay in early on, he was pulling deliveries off the stumps and nicking twos and threes. At the other end, Allan Border was playing very well and he finally had a word with Thommo. The number eleven started to play sensibly, leaving Border to play the strokes. He may have been out of form at that stage, but Border was one of the world's best batsmen. Ian Botham had helped get him back into form, by lending Border one of his Duncan Fearnley bats for that innings. That was typically sporting of Ian, but I began to get heartily sick of the sight of the 'DF' symbol as I stood behind Border! Soon Border looked dominant and Thommo took heart from him; they started to run some quick singles and we got a little ragged. We were trying to get at the number eleven batsman but Melbourne is such a big ground that they were running two to a fielder who was placed to save four but also was expected to keep them to a single. It may have looked as if we were giving Border the strike, but that was not so: some fielders were letting us down. The combination of left-hander and right-hander was also disconcerting.

The fourth day ended with Australia needing another 37 runs and England one wicket. More than 18,000 came to the ground, and were admitted free of charge for a day that could have been ended after just one ball. Overnight, we had concentrated on the vulnerability of Thomson. My theory was that he wasn't a number eleven batsman for nothing; sooner or later, his concentration would crack and he would play a loose shot. I stressed to our slips the need for complete concentration, because Thommo might chase a wide one and nick it. It was a dark, miserable morning, which placed extra pressure on our slips. At least I had the sightscreen with which to sight the ball, but our slips had to peer intently. We took the new ball early on that last morning, though it failed to do the trick. Some of our fielders were still a little slipshod and I handed out a few rollickings. Ian Botham came on for Norman Cowans without any immediate improvement and it began to look as if we had blown it. Just four runs needed and Bob Willis had to bowl at Allan Border, by now batting marvellously. Bob summoned up all his concentration and energy to bowl a magnificent maiden over at Border. He just couldn't get him away for a single, so Thommo had to face the next over. It was to be bowled by Ian Botham and off the first ball old 'golden arm' struck. The ball was about a foot wide of the off stump, Thommo fenced at it and it flew head height to Chris Tavaré at second slip. Tavaré was crouched down, he saw it late in the poor light and the ball burst his hands wide open. Luckily he got enough hand to the ball to force it upwards and backwards, giving Geoff Miller time to see it and run over from first slip to catch it. All credit to Geoff for keeping his wits about him and watching the ball. Next thing I knew was a war dance of delight from Botham and Willis, and Chris Tavaré and I ran off the pitch together, with Chris sighing with relief. The margin was just three runs. Instead of being three-nil down, the series score was now two-one.

The Aussies, as usual, took their defeat well while we tried to take it all in. Bob Willis looked absolutely drained and I was pleased for him; he would have picked up terrible flak for losing this one from such a good position, especially after putting them in at Adelaide and losing. His final over to Border, with the fielders at last closing in for each ball, was a masterpiece of control. I was delighted for Geoff Miller, so often the 'Nearly Man'. My heart went out to young Norman Cowans, a terrific lad who had worked very hard to get near the required standard in such a short space of time. Now he had won us the greatest game he was ever likely to play in. I even allowed myself a quiet purr of satisfaction: 37 runs in a tight spot in our second innings, five byes in the match on a wicket that kept low and a good, tumbling catch to get Kim Hughes when he lapped Geoff Miller and I had to change direction to get the deflection off his glove. It nearly went wrong for us, but cricket followers all over the world weren't complaining.

Anti-climax was at hand, and it came swiftly and cruelly. We needed an early breakthrough at Sydney in the final Test and we got it, except the umpire Mel Johnson didn't agree. Bob Willis ran out John Dyson in the first over off his own bowling, yet the umpire gave the batsman the benefit of the doubt. It was an amazing decision; the umpire didn't need to move from his square leg position and Dyson was a good two yards out. I felt we acquitted ourselves admirably in our public reaction to such an important mistake. Heaven knows what Abdul Qadir and Imran Khan would have done! Dyson went on to make 79 and we finished a rain-interrupted day fearing the worst. We never really got in the game, and on the fourth day, when the ball was turning, our spinners were just not tight enough to get the Aussies worrying. Kim Hughes and Allan Border helped themselves and played superbly. The variety provided by the slow left-arm of Edmonds might have been invaluable at that stage and I am sure the captain must have wondered what Edmonds might have made of the conditions.

So the Sydney Test petered out into a draw and I was batting when the game ended. I knelt down and kissed the ground, which raised a laugh or two. Sydney has always been a favourite ground of mine: nice people there, an enjoyable atmosphere and a pitch that often favours the spinners. I knew I was leaving the Sydney pitch for the last time as a player, so it seemed appropriate to say farewell in my usual sentimental manner.

After Sydney, the tour was an anti-climax for me. I didn't play after 11 January, yet the tour lasted a further five weeks. The Benson and Hedges World Series Cup games featured England,

Australia and New Zealand and I only managed a couple of appearances before Ian Gould displaced me for batting reasons. I just kicked my heels after that, I was bored to tears. It was a bad time for me. After doing the dogsbody work under Ray Illingworth 12 years previously, I was doing it again – not playing, humping cases around at airports while the younger players sat on their backsides. After we failed to qualify for the finals, we had to sit around for another fortnight in Sydney, waiting to go to New Zealand, to play three one-day internationals. As I knew I wouldn't be playing in New Zealand, I found myself thinking I would be better off at home, instead of trailing around. Nobody wanted to do any practice because the tour was effectively over, and there was a general air of indolence. The crazy itinerary and the fact that I was again out of contention because of my batting meant it was the worst month I have experienced on an England tour. It was different when I was understudy to Knott. I could respect his professionalism and genius. Ian Gould was less dedicated and not terribly successful as a batsman when he played in the internationals.

Ultimately a disappointing final tour of Australia for me. We were a little flattered still to be in contention right up to the final Test. I have to admit that Ian Botham was a big disappointment and I say that with the full knowledge of the wonderful things he has done for England. He seemed complacent at the start of the tour, taking little interest in practice. He talked about 'turning on the tap when I need to' but that ignored the fact that people like Greg Chappell, Kim Hughes and Geoff Lawson practised very hard, despite their success. All great players have a bad series and then we see their characters as they knuckle down to it in the nets and work their way back. Ian just fooled around in the nets and it was never 'alright on the night', despite some marvellous catching by him in the Tests. He didn't seem to understand that occupation of the crease is a great way to regain batting form, as Allan Border demonstrated from Melbourne onwards. Eventually Ian lost confidence with the bat, although he wouldn't admit it. As a bowler, he lacked peak fitness and as a keeper I could tell how much his action had changed since his great days. Due to excess weight, he wasn't turning round his shoulder to get side-on and his bouncers lacked venom. To this day, I don't know how much he is still troubled by his back that he injured in 1980, but he has certainly deteriorated as a bowler. It might have been better for Ian and the team if he had been dropped at some stage in Australia. He might then have been stung into getting himself fully fit, to rid him of any complacency. Ian was getting above the normal conventions of team selection, despite his undoubted brilliance in the past. We needed him at his best, but it was not there when he turned on the tap. Unlike Bob Willis, David Gower, Graham Gooch or myself, Ian has never been dropped by England and subconsciously hasn't had to motivate himself on occasions. We might have fared better in Australia if his pride had been hurt.

Despite the frustrations, there was one other memorable day for me on that Australian tour, and it came right at the start. On 24 October, I stumped Wayne Broad to make the 1,528th dismissal of my career. That passed J. T. Murray's record, so I was now statistically the most successful wicketkeeper of all time. I was especially pleased to reach it off the bowling of Geoff Miller, my county colleague, who had been a good friend for many years. He bowled one that went straight on, Broad played forward, dragged his toe and I stumped him. Nice to set the record straight with a stumping – always the keeper's pride and joy! I did a somersault of delight when the umpire gave the batsman out and everyone was very nice to me. Wayne Broad signed the press photo for me, the ball was engraved for me by the Queensland Cricket Association, and both mementoes from a happy day are now proudly displayed in my home.

I wanted to add as many victims as I could to my tally before I called it a day and I started the 1983 season in a positive frame of mind. I still wanted to be part of the England action for as long as my skills allowed, and my immediate aim was the Test series against New Zealand, and then the tour of Pakistan and New Zealand. I saw no room for me in the World Cup and they picked Ian Gould. Again I was surprised; I could see the need to have a wicketkeeper who could hit the ball hard and often and the best man for that was undoubtedly David Bairstow. He should have been in Australia with me the previous winter, with all those one-day games in the schedule, but he missed out. I reckon David has been unlucky over the years; a very good tourist, he knows his limitations, and will try his utmost to capitalise on his strengths. With him in the side, England might just have squeezed through to the World Cup final in 1983.

I regained my place for the Test series and thoroughly enjoyed the four Tests against a popular New Zealand side that was improving every year under the captaincy of Geoff Howarth. There was some splendid cricket played in a happy atmosphere. They bowled their overs at a commendably brisk rate, the startling success of Nick Cook meant I stood up to the stumps a fair amount and the cricket matched the beautiful weather. We won the series three-one and could look to the return series that winter with justifiable optimism.

Unfortunately everything went wrong on that tour. It was an anti-climactic way to end my England career. We lost both series, three players had to go home through illness or injury and we were dogged by controversy and speculation about off-field behaviour. I suppose the 1983–84 tour of New Zealand and Pakistan will go down in history as the Drugs Tour, even though the evidence for such activities crashed around the heads of the newspapers making the allegations. I saw no justification for the allegations at any time on the tour. The very idea of England players smoking pot during a rain interruption in a Test is absolutely ludicrous. I went to one of the Elton John concerts in New Zealand, where some of us allegedly smoked pot. I saw no evidence of that. Of course, the air was full of the stuff, it always is at such gatherings, but to my knowledge it had nothing to do with us. As far as I am concerned, our behaviour off the field was no worse than on any of my other tours. It is true that I spent less time with many of the players than on previous tours. For the first time I felt a distinct generation gap between myself and certain players who didn't share my views about cricket or life in general, but I could live with that. Invariably I would have a meal and a natter about old times with Bernard Thomas and our management team of Norman Gifford and Alan Smith. In New Zealand, there are more social distractions than in Pakistan and the team-room in the various hotels was not as fully visited as I would have liked. Ian Botham and Allan Lamb would want to get away from the environment of the team-room and drink in the hotel bar, but I couldn't see the point of that when we had free drink in the room. That was just a difference of opinion, a matter of contrasting values and not grounds for suspicion about some of our players. I took a very dim view of all the rumours. We were, after all, on the wrong end of a series defeat in New Zealand and I could just imagine the chat in the pubs back home, 'Look at that lot over there – all that money to play for England and they end up smoking pot.' Nobody representing his country could be happy with such a slur and I resented the implications. Whether the press speculation would have arisen if we had played well is another matter.

We didn't play well until really up against it in Pakistan, when the lads rallied round under David Gower and showed great determination. In New Zealand, we were very disappointing. We ought to have won the First Test at Wellington, but they rallied in their second innings as the wicket got flatter and flatter. The Second Test at Christchurch was a disaster from the start. In his first over Bob Willis sent careering over my head a ball that hit the boundary fence on the first bounce. After that, the wicket didn't behave too spitefully, although it always needed watching. It didn't stop New Zealand getting to 307 in even time, thanks to some marvellous hitting from Richard Hadlee and awful bowling from us. We needed a 'line and length' bowler, but the ideal man for that task, Neil Foster, had broken a bone in his foot during practice. Ian Botham obviously thought he just had to put the ball somewhere near the wickets and the pitch would do the rest. He went for five an over and bowled very unintelligently. They should have been out for about 120 and, when we went out to bat, we seemed to have it in our minds that the pitch was dangerous. The overhead conditions were worse when we batted, but we made it hard work. Richard Hadlee bowled as well as ever, using his brain, keeping the ball well up to the bat. They caught everything and got the luck at the right time. Having said all that, we were awful. It was the worst England performance of my time as a player and, to make matters worse, some of our team didn't seem all that perturbed as we were shot out for 82 and 93, to lose by an innings. Too many appeared happy enough to blame it on the wicket rather than examine their own shortcomings. When Bob Willis spoke to the media after the game, he talked too much about the state of the pitch, rather than our shortcomings. It sounded a little like sour grapes and he shielded his players from the public rocket we deserved. We had all played on similar wickets in England during our careers and we ought to have battled far harder. It didn't seem to hurt enough when we lost.

Having been handed that Test, the New Zealanders had no trouble in blocking out the Auckland Test to win their first series against us. All credit to them, but I hope I won't be accused of sounding unsporting when I say that only Geoff Howarth, John Wright and Richard Hadlee would have got into our team on merit. Yet they were integrated, they took whatever came their way and showed professionalism in finishing us off at Christchurch and keeping us at bay thereafter. We lacked their drive and pride.

We got some of that back in Pakistan, but not until we had gone one-down within a week of playing in New Zealand. There was too little time to acclimatise to the difficult conditions, but that was partly our fault, we had all wanted to spend as little time in Pakistan as possible and didn't complain at the itinerary. The tour began under threat of student riots and it looked as if the Karachi Test might not take place for a time. That didn't help us; I felt that the minds of some of our players weren't fully on the cricket. There was a feeling that the tour might be called off because the militia would be wading into the students too often to permit cricket. It was easier for the older ones like myself to say, 'It's a job of work, we've just got to concentrate on the cricket,' but, as a team, we just weren't ready for that First Test. We ran into the best spinner in the world, Abdul Qadir, a wily display of seam bowling from Sarfraz and some bad umpiring decisions that did us no favours at all. I was batting in the second innings with Nick Cook when he was given out, caught in the slips, when the ball was taken on the half volley. Nick stood his ground and let Mohsin Khan know what he thought about him and, although he was wrong to do that, I can understand his frustration. It happened to me shortly afterwards, when I was given out, caught off my pad. When they batted, needing just 65 to win, I caught Salim Malik, but that was not given. It wouldn't have made any difference, I suppose, although they only scraped home by three wickets. That was due to panic on their behalf. They always had the upper hand in that game. There was no point in moaning incessantly about the umpiring, because that would simply camouflage our defects. I was concerned at our slapdash attitude to fielding practice. It had been the same in New Zealand as well, and now we just had to snap out of it. I had always considered that fielding practice was the research work needed to graduate in a Test, yet some of our players clearly viewed it as a chore. At team meetings, I hammered home the point that high quality fielding was vital if we were to get a victory in Pakistan, where everything else was against us. The manager, A. C. Smith, and Bob Willis both took my side, but I got the feeling that some thought I was an old fuddy-duddy.

Soon we needed every ounce of our professionalism and team spirit. Ian Botham had to go home with knee trouble, then Bob Willis left, with suspected hepatitis. It was the best thing for both of them, but their departure, coupled with all the press rumours, meant we were in for a hard time. Then Graham Dilley had to go home, suffering from a mystery virus; cruel luck on him after he had found some splendid bowling form. Now we managed to pull ourselves together. The team-room, so denuded in New Zealand, was always full. We had to make our own entertainment to back up the videos of *Minder* that we seemed to know by heart. Graeme Fowler had bought an outrageously loud shirt, tie and hat in New Zealand and we announced a 'Wally of the Day' competition. The man who did the daftest thing that day had to wear the outfit at night; by the end of the tour, we all had had a stint with it. Sounds silly perhaps, but little things like that kept us going. David Gower batted very well indeed when replacing Bob Willis as captain and we regained some pride and played with a good deal more common sense. David's increased confidence with the bat transferred itself into his captaincy and I felt he was assertive enough in the last two Tests. Mike Gatting, a man with a good cricket brain and a good motivator, backed him up well as vice-captain and we did as well as could be expected with such a depleted side. We didn't square the series, but did ourselves justice and came out of it with honour after such a disastrous start. None of us were really well at any stage of the Pakistan leg of the tour, so it was a good effort to come back in the last two Tests.

As we flew back home at the end of March, I had a sneaking suspicion that it might be my last England tour, though I still wanted to carry on as long as my form and fitness lasted. The papers reported me as saying that I couldn't wait for the tour to finish, that I was critical of the attitude of some of my colleagues. The latter remark was true, but I didn't lose my keenness to play in Pakistan, I was as committed as ever. It wasn't such a happy tour as previous ones and that wasn't because we had lost. The lack of dedication from some of my team-mates disturbed me. Defeat wasn't a jolt to them, they seemed to think it could be easily dismissed and that a few beers later it would be history. I felt sorry for Bob Willis as he tried to stamp down on such blasé attitudes and, after a time, it occurred to me that he and I seemed to be the only ones who really got hurt by defeat. It was no coincidence that we were the two oldest players in the party: the generation gap had suddenly begun to look very wide.

CHAPTER 11

THE FASCINATION OF TOURING

In my career, I went on 12 official tours – nine of them with England – and I can honestly say that I enjoyed them all, irrespective of what happened on the pitch. My last two England tours had their playing frustrations, but the fascination of being on the other side of the world never left me. Some cricketers get terribly homesick on tour and allow that to mar their enjoyment; now no one missed his home and family more than me, but I always felt that these trips were part of life, an experience not to be missed. I never saw the point in moping about in a faraway hotel, counting the days before the plane took us home to Blighty. To me, it was a case of making the best of things, to be positive and try to broaden one's mind. It was a privilege to be sent on a cricket tour and I have hoarded some priceless memories that had little to do with the actual play. In my time on tour, I have met Mother Theresa of Calcutta, watched a James Bond film in Urdu, drunk lager from a teapot to avoid police suspicions in the 'dry state' of Pakistan, talked to convicted murderers in a Sri Lankan jail, and observed Geoff Boycott wangle some champagne out of a British Prime Minister. I have been robbed in Jamaica, frightened out of my wits by a giant rat in India and experienced the difficulties of breaking down racial barriers in a Rest of the World side.

My visit to Mother Theresa occupies pride of place in my memories. I had long admired her selfless dedication to the poor in Calcutta and, when I finally made a full England tour to India, I nourished the faint hope that I might meet her. It came on the rest day of the Calcutta Test in January 1982. The High Commission kindly arranged the visit and about 12 of us went along at seven-thirty in the morning, the only time she could see us. She entered the room, a small, bird-like figure of nearly 80, and greeted us charmingly. When we told her why we had come to

121

India, she smiled and attempted a bowling action. Eventually half of us went to see the orphanage and the others to the hospital run by Mother Theresa. We let the girls go and see the children and I went along to the hospital. It was a harrowing sight: it turned out to be the place where the dying are taken off the streets of Calcutta, where they spend their last peaceful hours on Earth. The air was thick with disinfectant and the unmistakeable smell of death and I was almost sick. Just as I thought I was going to pass out, a large nun shoved a smock at me and said, 'Come on, help us feed them.' With the best will in the world, I just couldn't face it; neither could Bernard Thomas, and he's a medical man! Luckily Bernard's wife and Ann Subba Row came to the rescue and fed some of the poor souls as we watched. I started chatting with an Australian girl, who I assumed was training to be a nun. She said she had come there from Brisbane a few months earlier, but was about to go back home and resume her normal life as a nurse. I thought that was wonderful: she couldn't be a nun by vocation, but she still felt she had to do something with Mother Theresa, and for humanity. We left after having our pictures taken with Mother Theresa. It was all very humbling and, predictably, I couldn't eat a thing when we got back to our usual plush existence at the hotel. I tried to get some of our tour sponsorship money handed over to Mother Theresa, but it was too complicated, so I waited until we returned to England. Cathy and I organised some fund-raising at our local church, and Cathy joined a committee aimed at raising funds for eye operations for children out in India. That visit made me count my blessings and realise what it was like to be in the presence of someone with the qualities of a saint. She had this quiet charisma that was so moving. And all we had to worry about was the Indian umpires and flat wickets!

Later on that tour, I came face to face with some murderers. It was at Kandy, in Sri Lanka, and the irrepressible Ian Botham was responsible for this slice of low life. Now Ian has many redeeming qualities, but he has a fairly ghoulish sense of humour. On tour, he is never still, he always wants to know what's going on away from the cricket. His thirst for adventure takes him into some unlikely places and none more so than the prison we visited. Neither of us were playing in the game at Kandy and Ian had heard about the nearby prison. 'Come on, let's go and look at the murderers,' he said to me. I could think of more entrancing prospects, but I was whisked along. We were made very welcome at the prison and had a quick look around. Ian asked to see the murderers and soon we were staring at them through the bars, the whole place smelling of urine. Just as I thought we were going to get out of the place, Ian piped up, 'Do you hang them here?' On being told that it was no longer practised he asked, 'Have you still got the scaffold here? Can we see it?' I didn't know why he kept saying 'we' – I didn't want to see any of it! So we were shown the scaffold. I took just a passing look, but, of course, Ian wanted to know all the ins and outs of the hanging process. He asked about the way they judge the height and weight of the condemned man and was suitably impressed by the answers. 'Can you open the trapdoor?' he asked, and stood there looking at the drop and visualising the grizzly scene. I couldn't wait to go, but Ian wanted to know more. The prison superintendent told us a story about a prisoner who was due to die, but heard that the Queen was about to visit the island. That brought the prospect of hanging being abolished, so to play for time until Her Majesty's arrival the prisoner slit his stomach open. The medical treatment he needed delayed his execution and, by the time he had recovered, hanging had been abolished. My stomach was turning over at the story, but not Ian's. 'Can we see this bloke?' Well, he was wheeled out, along with a couple of others, and none of them could speak a word of English. That didn't bother Ian: an interpreter was on hand and he asked to see the scars on the prisoner's stomach. It seems he had killed six men in self-defence after drinking some moonshine liquor. He took a cleaver to his victims and I could tell Ian was mightily impressed by all this. Finally – to my intense relief – the grizzly visit was over and Ian chattered excitedly about it all the way back to the ground. He made sure the lads heard about it as well! A few months later, and there was an ironic sting in the tail. The prisoner who flourished the cleaver to such telling effect wrote to me, saying he was very sorry for what he had done. I wrote back to him; after all he had taken the trouble to contact me and he must have been hoping I would get him out. Ian didn't get a letter though. As I said to him, 'You ask the questions, but I get the letter!'

Ian Botham has an indestructible appetite for life and food, but even he was made to feel queasy once on that tour. On the rest day of the Kanpur Test, he and Keith Fletcher went to shoot duck on the Ganges. The hotel had provided them with a picnic lunch and all seemed to be going smoothly, as their bearer punted them down the river in search of duck. All of a sudden, Ian spotted a dead body, then another, and another. Huge fish were feeding off the bodies. Our two heroes then realised that the Ganges was a holy river, that bodies are deposited in the river through religious reverence. They could just about stomach all that, until it came to lunch. While they nervously wondered if they could manage to keep down their lunch amid all the dead bodies and swollen fish, their bearer got stuck into his with great relish. After he had finished off his curry, he dipped the empty bowl into the river and drank out of it! I don't know whether the corpses and the puffed-up fish gave the water extra flavour, but even Ian Botham missed out on his food that day!

He had his leg unmercifully pulled about that one, but Ian had already enjoyed a good laugh at my expense earlier on, at Nagpur. Nagpur is situated right in the centre of India. It is called Snake City for obvious reasons and not even a patriot would call it the loveliest part of that fascinating country. It was early in the tour and we had been primed with all sorts of horror stories about rats and snakes in that part of India. We were staying in a rest home and having to come to terms with the fact that there were no toilet rolls, soap or blankets, even though the authorities had known for months that we were coming. We were allocated rooms in bungalows and Bernard Thomas, Derek Underwood and I were sharing one of them. It was a pretty uninspiring sight: the fans were whirring, paint was peeling off the walls and a 60-watt bulb meant we were straining our eyes as we tried to read. Suddenly we heard a scratching noise and a massive rat struggled under the door. It was about eight inches long and had squeezed through a gap of about two inches. It ran along the skirting board and, when I threw my book at it, it went back the way it had entered the room. 'There you are, I told you,' said Derek, who had regaled us with stories from his two previous trips to India. I was shaken out of my wits, but had calmed down by the time we went to bed. We all retired to our individual rooms and I climbed into bed and remembered to tuck the mosquito net around the bed. Just my luck – I had to go to the toilet, the perennial problem of an Indian tour. I staggered outside to the tiny toilet, keeping my eyes open all the time. As I sat on the toilet – pyjama bottoms round my feet – I heard a squeaking noise. The same rat raced over my feet. My hair literally stood on end and I nearly hit the ceiling. The rat jumped up and scuttled back into the hole. I bunged up the hole with a Coke bottle and when I returned to my room jammed cricket socks and newspapers under the door to keep the rat away. I left the light on all night, and didn't sleep a wink. We christened him Roddy the Rat and the other lads shuddered at the story. Keith Fletcher – who had toured India twice – felt vindicated by the tale and proceeded to tell me a hairy story about the bats of Hyderabad. On his last trip to Pakistan, Fletch went into dinner in the hotel at Hyderabad. It was very steamy and he switched on the fans in the dining-room. Unknown to him, that upset the bats who were sleeping on the ceiling; the fans cut them to pieces and bits of shredded bat kept dropping into the soup as the lads ate their dinner! Ian Botham liked that one.

Actually, Ian and I had experienced the charms of Hyderabad on our tour of Pakistan in 1977–78. Hyderabad is in the middle of the Sind desert and not exactly an ideal holiday spot. The hotel we stayed at was a dreadful place, and the facilities at the ground were hardly any better. Geoff Boycott had to strip on the toilet because there wasn't enough space in the dressing-room. A thin partition divided the toilet from our dressing-room and the stench was awful. When the day's play ended – and remember this was a Test match – we would all head straight back to the hotel at four-thirty. We would be sweating buckets, the dust would have made us very thirsty and we would then try to wash off some of the grime. That was difficult – in the hotel bathrooms there was a tap on the wall about two feet from the floor and we had to crouch down and sprinkle handfuls of water over ourselves. That was our shower after a day's toil in a Test! The rest day in that Hyderabad Test was an instructive experience. We had been given VIP tickets to go to the local cinema, a big treat considering what passed for entertainment around those parts. Well, the cinema turned out to be a bug-hutch and the James Bond film had a soundtrack in Urdu. As soon as we got there, the locals had to be bundled out of the VIP seats for the Englishmen, which caused a commotion. When we settled down to try to follow the film we couldn't cope with the deafening volume. Phil Edmonds shouted, 'Turn the bloody sound down!' and got out of his seat to make his point clear to the projectionist. When he did turn down the volume, everyone else in the cinema started complaining because it was too low. Somehow our eardrums survived the experience!

That Pakistan tour was the only one in which Ian Botham was laid low. He was very poorly for a long time with dysentery and by his standards he was subdued. That didn't stop him from crowing about his food parcels from home, though. Ian had been one of the lucky ones – mine arrived in New Zealand after being waylaid by Customs – and he gloated over the tins of paté sent by his wife. Eventually he was prevailed upon to share them out; after all, he was supposed to be ill. Drink was even more of a problem, because Pakistan was a dry state. We encountered a novel way of getting round the restrictions in Rawalpindi. An English supporter invited us to a Chinese restaurant. After a time, he said, 'May I suggest we have some special tea?' We would have given anything for a pint of English bitter, but we agreed without any great show of enthusiasm. The teapot was brought to the table and our host poured. We were rather surprised to see froth coming out of the teapot's mouth. It was lager! Our host winked conspiratorially and we tucked in with gusto. True to form, the bragging about Chinese tea didn't go down too well in the team-room with the others that night!

As you might expect, Geoffrey Boycott found a more privileged way of getting a drink in Pakistan. At the Lahore Test, the then British Prime Minister, Mr James Callaghan, came to see us at the ground. We were lined up and introduced to him and I was standing near to Boycott when I heard him ask the Prime Minister for some champagne. Mr Callaghan said he would see what he could do. The High Commissioner pulled some strings and Boycs got his champers. He did the same with General Zia later in the tour. On each occasion, I don't know how many bottles he managed to get, because I never saw any of it.

Although every England cricketer has his share of horror stories from tours to the Indian sub-continent, it must be said that things have got better in my time. The 1983–84 tour of Pakistan was a big improvement in terms of accommodation, food and drink, compared with 1977–78. To be fair, they did their best to make us welcome and some of the hotels were excellent. In India, I stayed in some hotels that were superior to anything I've ever seen throughout the world. The problem comes when you play in parts of Pakistan and India where there is little commercial activity. Places like Hyderabad, Kanpur and Nagpur are a true test of character and, in their own way, help to foster team spirit. You find yourself appreciating your teammates and enjoying the fun that comes from providing your own entertainment. Charades proves to be a very popular game in such circumstances!

The climactic demands of a tour are often a challenge to the resolve of a professional sportsman. The dust of the Indian sub-continent is a big problem, especially to someone like Geoffrey Boycott, who wore contact lenses. On my last tour of Pakistan, we were all groggy at various times with sore throats aggravated by the dust. You just have to grit your teeth and battle through. I remember the state I was in between the Calcutta and Madras Tests of 1982. I went ahead of the others with Keith Fletcher and Bernard Thomas because I wasn't feeling all that well. Eventually I became delirious and spent three hours in a darkened room at the airport, waiting for the flight to Madras. The doctor said I was dehydrated and there seemed little chance of recovering for the next Test in three days' time. Somehow I managed it, and kept pretty well. I even got a bowl as the game petered out into a draw! My experience at Madras was just an example of what we face when we play cricket in India and Pakistan. I have seen Bob Willis so tired after a whole night of stomach trouble that he could hardly lift his eyelids, but he still went out there and bowled his hardest. At Madras, Ian Botham sweated a whole night away with a nasty virus infection, but he forced himself to bowl the next day. You have to accept the lows with the highs, they are part of the job.

I had to come to terms with a different problem in Australia when I toured with the Rest of the World side in 1971-72. For some reason, early in the tour the white players in that squad couldn't get through to the non-whites. We just never saw them other than at grounds. They took taxis together, socialised together and kept away from us. Even Garry Sobers, our captain, took no part in socialising with the white members of his team. It was crazy: we were due to play in front of 50,000 people against Australia, and we had no team spirit, no team-room. I tried hard to split them up, by sitting between the Indians, Bishan Bedi and Sunil Gavaskar, in a taxi, but they didn't seem too pleased at that. None of the white players could understand why people like Zaheer Abbas, Rohan Kanhai, Garry Sobers, Clive Lloyd, Bishan Bedi and Intikhab Alam kept away from us socially, when we saw them regularly in English county cricket. At last we hit on an idea to break down the barriers. Norman Gifford, Richard Hutton and I decided to form a 'Saturday night club', a fairly normal touring device, where the players meet for an hour on that night and get a lot of drink down their throats. We pinned up a notice, saying that there would be a meeting in the room occupied by Hutton and Gifford and we stipulated what was required: everyone had to wear a white jockstrap, a black sock and have a comb in their hair. The reference to a comb was my way of having a dig at Farokh Engineer, who kept borrowing mine. This way, he would have to buy one at last! We stocked up the bar for the arrival of the others and it was terrific watching them walk into the room, wearing just a jockstrap and one sock. They all had to use the stairs or the lift to get up to the hotel room, so they must have been given some strange looks. Garry Sobers laughed himself silly at the scene and it helped to break some of the ice – but unfortunately we had miscalculated over the drink. Some of the Asians like Zaheer and Gavaskar didn't drink for religious reasons, and they didn't take too kindly to us trying to get them sozzled. Yet it all worked out when we next tried it. The two South Africans, Tony Greig and Hylton Ackerman, hadn't heard of a 'Saturday night club' before and they loved it. They mixed the drinks for the next session in Perth and they instituted a fines system if anyone failed to finish their drinks. They didn't tell us that they had also laced the drinks! As a result, we were well and truly sozzled fairly easily and at the end of an hour Zaheer and Gavaskar were seasoned drinkers. Team spirit picked up dramatically, we all pitched into the taxis without thinking about colour and we started to play very well. It turned out to be a happy, harmonious tour – but to this day I don't know why it started off on the wrong foot.

As professional sportsmen, cricketers inevitably get embroiled in politics whether they like it or not. I noticed this in South Africa, when I toured there in 1976 with the International Wanderers team under the managership of Richie Benaud. Our aim was to promote multi-racial cricket in South Africa and I believe we did an excellent job in that respect. John Shepherd was the only black player in our party and it was interesting to see that in some areas he was not welcomed by the non-whites. They clearly felt that John had sold out to the white man by coming on that tour. I roomed with John and I know that he felt uncomfortable when four of us had to go to an exclusive public school in Johannesburg to address the pupils. Richie Benaud, Ian Chappell, John and myself had to be there at eight o'clock in the morning and when we stepped on stage we were greeted by an amazing sight. There must have been 2,000 people in the hall – the pupils were immaculately dressed, their parents were also in their Sunday best while the teachers were sporting their gowns and mortar boards. It was all terribly formal and my heart sank when we were asked to say a few words individually. It was no problem to Richie and Ian but Shep and I were out of our depth. John was the only black man there and he seemed ill at ease, not surprisingly. I have to say that on that tour I felt less animosity towards the black man than I have done in places like Jamaica or Guyana.

I shan't forget the time I was robbed in broad daylight in Jamaica. It was in 1974, when black power was sweeping the Caribbean, and we had been warned not to step out of our hotel in Kingston. Within half an hour, I had completely forgotten the warning as I realised I was right out of airmail letters, so I nipped out to get some. The shop was just 200 yards from the hotel and, when I came out of it, I found myself surrounded by four large Jamaicans. I could see the hotel in the distance, but it was a case of so near yet so far. I thought to myself, 'I'm in trouble here,' which was hardly the most perceptive notion of my life. One of them said, 'Have you got any Jamaican dollars? We're students and we want to buy books.' Luckily I had just about a pound's worth of dollars and I handed them over. They realised that was all I had and they let me go. I sprinted my way back to the hotel, grateful that Bob Chat had talked his way out of trouble!

Such an incident was a rare cloud on my horizon while touring. It's been a privilege to travel the world as an England player – to savour the oysters in New Zealand, the fish and delicious wines of Australia, to explore the fabulous delights of India and to marvel at the lush greenery of Sri Lanka. My career has led me to places like Penang, Kashmir and the Taj Mahal, and spoiled me for holidays to take when I'm not on a cricket tour. I wouldn't have missed any of those 12 tours for anything and I only wish I could start all over again. Truly the game has taken me a long way from Bignall End.

SOME PERSONALITIES OF MY TIME

In my time on the world cricket scene, I have witnessed many great players at first hand. Apart from the World Cup final of 1979, I never really got to close quarters with the West Indians. My tour over there in 1973–74 was spent as understudy to Alan Knott, while appearances in county cricket do not yield a deep insight into their great players. Apart from that, I have seen a great deal of all the other world-class cricketers of the last two decades. Here is my assessment of some of them, plus a look at one or two players who have been either great friends or interesting characters.

Geoff Boycott

Geoffrey Boycott comes under the heading of great player and interesting character, but not friend. I found it very hard to get anywhere near to Boycott – he seemed to feel that he had to keep proving himself. Maybe it was due to his upbringing, but he wasn't the only one who had to struggle early on from working-class origins. Time after time, he would be difficult and uncommunicative. Only Mike Brearley ever seemed to get through to him, a fact that probably annoyed Boycott more than most things. It was no secret that Boycott felt he should have been given the England captaincy once he ended his self-imposed exile in 1977 and turned down Kerry Packer. Yet Mike was far superior as a captain, a point underlined when he had to go home after breaking his arm on the tour of Pakistan and New Zealand in 1977–78 and Boycott, the vice-captain, took over.

When we got to New Zealand, it was clear that Boycs was wound up about being captain as well as our best batsman. I think he took the responsibilities far too seriously and in my view his behaviour also left a lot to be desired. During the Wellington debacle, when we lost for the first time to New Zealand, he was guilty of a bad piece of public relations in front of the England players and many spectators. Richard Collinge had bowled him, playing an uncharacteristically loose shot, and he walked back to the pavilion in a fury. A schoolboy of about eight years of age chose the wrong time to ask for his autograph as he stalked back. Boycott pushed him aside as he walked up the pavilion steps, and gave the boy a few well-chosen words for good measure. Of course the boy might have chosen a better time but there was no excuse for such behaviour from the England captain. The lad almost fell over and he started to cry because he had been embarrassed. We were sitting in deckchairs outside the pavilion and witnessed the whole sorry episode, and Bernard Thomas had the presence of mind to defuse the situation. Bernard went inside with the autograph book, made sure that Boycott signed and half an hour later Boycott came out to apologise to the youngster.

In the next Test at Christchurch, he again buckled under the responsibilities of captain. We just failed to make them follow on and I noticed some heads were starting to drop in the field. I said to Boycs, 'Come on, keep going – just one more wicket to get and we've still got a good lead'; he flared up at me and said, 'You **** off back behind the wicket and leave it to me,' and I snapped back, 'Well, do it yourself then.' He didn't seem to realise that I was simply trying to gee everyone up and encourage the captain. Worse was to follow. When we needed quick runs in the second innings, Boycott batted as if all the cares of the world were on his shoulders. We sat seething in the dressing-room, knowing that quick runs were crucial to give us a day to bowl them out. Ian Botham said, 'Don't worry, I'll sort it out,' and sure enough he did so when it was his turn to bat. He ran Boycott out quite blatantly and proceeded to smash some much-needed runs. Boycott came back to the dressing-room in a fury, lay down, put a towel around his head and ignored us. Phil Edmonds asked him if he should go in next to smash some quick runs and the captain of England replied, 'You can please yourself what you do.' It was left to Bob Willis as vice-captain to sort out the rest of the batting order. The following morning, Boycott had snapped out of his sulk, but was very indecisive about a declaration. It was obvious to all of us that we needed to declare overnight, on a flat wicket against useful batsmen, but Kenny Barrington, our manager, had to talk him into it. In the end, magnificent bowling won us the game, but the captain gets no credit for that from me. At that time, his friends in the press were fanning the flames about the England captaincy, but no other player on that tour would have preferred him to Brearley and I imagine Kenny's tour report made interesting reading.

I admire Boycott as a professional cricketer. As a fellow-member of the 'Golden Oldies', I respect the way he has kept himself fit and his dedicated attitude to net practice. Never the most gifted of batsmen, he realised that he had to function at his very best to chisel out the runs and he set himself to combine full concentration with great application. If you could have grafted on Boycott's professionalism to Gower's strokeplay, you would then have the complete batsman, and I think that Boycott secretly admired the gifts of Botham, Gooch and Gower. Having paid tribute to his determination, it must be said that he didn't do himself any favours over the years. He seemed to think the whole world was against him and he had this desperate need to have people fuss over him. At Sydney in 1980, he had to be persuaded to play by Mike Brearley. The wicket had been soaked by rain, the start had been delayed and the teams were due to be named when Boycott announced that he had some minor ailment and couldn't play. Some of our lads hit the roof and told him not to be so stupid. I don't believe for one moment that Boycott was physically afraid of batting against Lillee on a tricky wicket – it was more a fear of failure that bothered him. Yet even if he wasn't fully fit, he had to play because he was our best batsman and his defensive skill was vital. As poor Wayne Larkins stood there, not knowing whether or not he was in, Mike Brearley talked Boycott round. I don't believe anyone else could have done that.

Boycott's withdrawal from Test cricket for three years also stemmed from a need to be appreciated. His magnificent batting in West Indies in 1973–74 probably helped keep Mike Denness in the job as England captain for the forthcoming Australian tour, and Boycott absented himself, blaming mental pressure. He must have fancied the England job, because he was Yorkshire captain at the time. I don't believe he was worried about the quick Aussie bowlers – he has never been physically scared – but I think he wanted people to ask him back. He wanted to keep in the limelight, to have people say, 'Geoff, we really missed you out there. If only you had been opening for England, we wouldn't have been slaughtered.' For some reason he seemed to need regular public boosts to his ego and the press were only too happy to oblige.

He has annoyed me many times with some strange behaviour. When I motored down to Lord's in 1981 to wish the England lads all the best for the West Indies tour and to get some bats signed for my testimonial, I guessed I might have trouble with Geoff. I had seen him playing the Scarlet Pimpernel at many such functions at Lord's just before a tour; he is never around for very long, he keeps disappearing and seems to love to have people running around looking for him. I had no problems at all with any of the other lads, but Boycott was, as usual, elusive. After three hours of hanging around, I left without his signature on the bats. The following day, I spent two hours tracing his autograph onto the bats. I knew that the first person to win the bat in a raffle would say, 'Boycott's name isn't on it.' That's the effect he seems to have on so many people – partly due to favourable press coverage over the years, partly due to his towering achievements.

When he went home from the Indian tour in 1982, I thought he had burned his boats with England – irrespective of his three-year ban for his involvement with South Africa. I am sure that Lord's has now marked his card and that his reinstatement would be felt likely to undermine the captain. As a batsman, he is probably still good enough to play for England at the age of 45, although he is now a little slower in the field. The game must be bigger than any individual. Before his South African adventure, I thought Boycott was mapping out his career very nicely. He did a good job as occasional summariser on BBC television and I thought he would walk into a job with them once he retired. It was typical of the man's attention to detail that he used to tape his commentaries and examine them for faults afterwards. He used to say to me, 'Did you hear me the other day? Did I come over well?' Again the need to be appreciated.

I don't believe that Geoff will sit under a shady tree in South Africa when he retires. Yorkshiremen are a breed apart in cricket, and I think he will dedicate himself to becoming the top dog in the county. Yorkshire cricketers seem to believe they have missed out on something if they leave the county and I think Boycott would miss all the wheeling and dealing that goes on up there.

I think I am better placed than most to judge Boycott as a batsman, since I must have bowled more at him in the nets than anyone else. He was always very cute about that; Botham would blast all the bowlers into oblivion in the nets, so that eventually no one wanted to bowl at him, but Boycott treated us all with respect so he could get a long session out of us. My medium-pace rubbish was treated with great suspicion, so I had a good chance to admire his impeccable technique and the way he could get into a smooth rhythm. He would concentrate on one shot for an age, perfecting it. Then he would work on another. A great professional with a bat in his hands.

Mike Brearley

Mike Brearley was almost a complete contrast to Boycott in life style, as captain and in his judgement of the outside world. I always felt he was a better bat than his critics acknowledged, as a glance at his career record will confirm. Mike lost the crucial batting years (between 25 and 30) because of his desire to pursue his academic career, yet this awareness that there was more to life than cricket was one of his greatest strengths. Not that he didn't try as batsman or captain – it was simply a case that he brought a broad perspective to the game and wouldn't be dogged by suspicion and orthodoxy. Mike would never be afraid to try things and his coolness was marvellous. I can't think of anyone better to mastermind those escape acts at Headingley and Edgbaston in 1981, but even when we were losing – as in Australia in 1979–80 – I never felt that we were out of control. If Mike couldn't pull it off, then no one could.

Mike has been the only one to handle Boycott and Botham properly – Boycott through quiet cajolery and Botham through a mixture of leg-pulling and firm leadership. He would let Ian brood and smoulder for just long enough, then crack down on him when it was time to get involved again. I think Ian respected him for his skill in handling people and also for his luck. To a certain extent, Mike made his own luck by his mental flexibility, but there is no doubt that he possessed that enviable gift of fortune. It was strange that he could handle such characters as Boycott and Botham, but he could never come to terms with Phil Edmonds. For some reason, Phil could always wind Mike up: Phil seemed to think that Mike wasn't the only man in the squad with a Cambridge degree and he would be rather assertive about that. Mike would sometimes fly off the handle at Phil, even though a man of his intellect and psychological depth should surely have realised that Edmonds was just trying to rile him. I suppose every man has his blind spots and Edmonds was certainly one with Mike.

134

I was always impressed at the way Mike handled players who lacked his intellectual accomplishments. He would never talk down to us, never indulge in name-dropping or flaunt his posh books around, while we sat reading *The Sun* or the *Mirror*. I once experienced this thoughtfulness when he invited me out to John Inverarity's house in Adelaide. I knew John from his tours of England and Mike asked if I would come along with him. I agreed, only to find myself involved in a dinner party where the talk was highly intellectual and way above my head. As a school teacher himself, John Inverarity had invited people of his mental calibre and I'm afraid I soon discovered that I wasn't on any of their wavelengths. Mike saved the situation for me; noticing that I was quiet at the dinner table, he kept bringing me into the conversations in which I could make a contribution, and whenever somebody started another intellectual dialogue, Mike would steer the conversation back to more mundane matters. Of course, I was Mike's responsibility, because he had invited me to the dinner, but it was typically thoughtful of him to take care of me.

I admired his strength of character on the 1979–80 tour of Australia. For some reason, Mike had to represent the views of the TCCB on things like coloured clothing, fielding circles and night cricket – instead of Lord's sending someone out there to do all the committee work. Very soon, Mike acquired the reputation of the Whingeing Pom who was far too posh for the Aussies. The crowds gave him some awful abuse, but he never buckled and, indeed, batted very well on that tour. In private, Mike wasn't over-diplomatic to some influential Aussies who he suspected of sharp practice on that tour – but his public reserve and unflappability never wavered.

A complex character, Mike. I've seen him stand his ground in a Test and refuse to walk, even though everyone knew he had snicked the ball – yet his honesty robbed Geoff Cope of a hat-trick in Cope's first Test. At Lahore in 1977, Iqbal Qasim was on his way back to the pavilion, convinced he had been caught at slip by Brearley to give Cope three wickets in three balls. Mike thought better of it, decided that the ball hadn't carried and called the batsman back. I thought Mike would have known the truth as soon as he gathered the ball, rather than wait for the congratulations to begin. Still he knew best – the dominant reaction of most players who have been captained by this pleasant, impressive man.

Ian Botham

Ian Botham has been the most brilliant natural cricketer of my England career and, at times, the most infuriating. Ian just won't accept that he is no longer the bowler of his prime: that golden period between New Zealand early in 1978 and the Bombay Jubilee Test in 1980. His force of personality has given him too many overs in recent years when he should have been standing at slip, helping the captain spot things for the good of the side. I feel Ian has been an ordinary bowler since 1982: the zip is there occasionally, but too often that massive body isn't sideways on when he delivers the ball. Ian also seems to labour under the delusion that you get class batsmen out by bouncers. That may be so if you are as quick as Malcolm Marshall, but Ian's reduced pace in recent years has been meat and drink to the best players. His whole make-up is geared towards attack and I think a maiden over bores Ian as much as anything. He still gathers in his share of wickets, but they now cost too much and he rarely keeps it tight when a quiet period is needed.

He is stubborn about his bowling and stubborn about his captaincy. He just won't accept that his form suffered during those Tests in 1980 and 1981 because he was leading England. He still maintains that he wants to be captain again before his career ends. I just don't know why: Ian's attitude in the nets isn't professional, he doesn't relish the public relations chores that come with the job and he prides himself on his blunt speaking. Temperamentally, I feel Ian lacks the coolness of thought to be a good captain. He is one of those who likes to lead from the front, to go over the top with all guns blazing – yet sometimes a captain has to retrench and gain some breathing space.

I wish he would get the captaincy thing out of his system, because he still has so much to offer. Despite his facade of unconcern, Ian is a very good analyst of cricketers. At our pre-Test dinners, he was always first-class at spotting technical things about the opposition and he could dissect the weaknesses very impressively. He is modest about his own performances and is quick to praise those with far less talent. A genuine team man, Ian never glories in his achievements and just lets his record speak for itself. We always felt he was a great man to have on our side and his guts and determination were fantastic. He must have a very high pain threshold: time after time he has bowled through injuries or illness on tour and never complained. He always wants to be in the game and will accept responsibility. He may be foolishly cavalier on occasions, but that's the way he plays. I think his batting could be even greater if he could accept the decline in his bowling. He has given tantalising glimpses of batting greatness – particularly in India in 1981–82 – and he is a great sight when playing properly. The bat comes down in a straight line, the head remains still and his off-side driving is beautifully correct. Ian is equally good off front and back foot and he is one of the few players around who can be guaranteed to score quickly. Even in Tests, his striking rate per hour is tremendous; not many players can score at such a rate and still look safe, but Ian can when he's really concentrating.

I don't think I've seen a greater catcher of the ball in any position in the field. His catching technique is, like the man himself, highly individualistic and should not be copied. When I coach youngsters the elements of fielding I always say to them, 'Never stand like Ian Botham, with hands on knees as the ball hits the bat. He is a genius and makes his own rules.' He sees the ball so early – another plus factor in his batting – and as a result can get his hands off his knees in time, but lesser mortals have to rely on the tried and tested technique of cupping the hands in front of them. As an allround fielder, Ian is marvellous. For a big bloke he is very quick to the ball and his tremendous competitiveness makes him alive to the possibility of run-outs and turning twos into ones.

When I sit and think about Ian's allround accomplishments I again realise what a wonderful cricketer he has been and what a pleasure it was to play alongside him. I just hope that he can still keep it going, but I worry about his mental attitude. When I used to chide him about looking after his fitness, he would grin and call me 'OAP', for obvious reasons, but I was genuinely concerned for him. He has needed a break from cricket for several years now, and I hope he'll still be around for a long time. I'm very fond of the guy, and wish him well. He must have put more backsides on seats than any other English cricketer since Denis Compton.

Bob Willis

Bob Willis has been one of Ian's closest friends in cricket, but they were poles apart in temperament and attitude to the game. Bob was often rather negative about our chances – he had a long grievance about the quality of England's batting – and he tended to fear the worst, while Ian would expect us to prosper if we looked on the bright side. Bob took the game of cricket very seriously and triumphed through force of will. Only Boycott spent more time psyching himself up for the big games and he would often appear to be from another planet when bowling. He had to change his approach when made England captain; no longer could he switch off and graze down at third man. Bob had to do his best at mid-on or mid-off and be on hand for a tactical word. I think he did as well as one could expect from a 33-year-old fast bowler. It took a lot to swallow his resentment at the media and present himself at those interminable press conferences before, during and after a Test match. A natural worrier, he took things to heart and sometimes blew things out of proportion. I just wish others had tried as hard as the captain to make light of our defeats after the South African episode robbed us of so many fine players in 1982. On our last England tour together, I got the distinct impression that we were the only two still brooding about a defeat several hours later. Many of the others seemed to think a few beers would blow away all the memories.

It was all a far cry from our first tour, in Australia under Ray Illingworth. When Bob flew out after a month to replace Alan Ward he was an instant hit. He had a nice confident way about him that could never be interpreted as cockiness; he just fitted in straight away and drank in all the tips offered by so many senior players. I roomed with him for a time and he knew he was a greenhorn but made no secret of his desire to learn and to be a better cricketer. He was a star on the team coach: he seemed to know every dirty ditty that could ever have been sung in a rugby club. Everyone took to him. As a fast bowler he was sharp enough, but I would never have believed that 13 years later he would still be smacking the ball into my gloves with over 300 Test wickets to his credit.

Bob's single-minded approach made him a great Test bowler, but the strain also took it out of him and affected his county career. He often found it hard to relax during a cricket season or on tour, because – like Boycott – he felt he had to be in the right frame of mind to make everything count when he was called on. It was gratifying that his bowling held up under the extra burden of the England captaincy. I had wondered whether he would struggle, but he did very well with the ball. Indeed, I doubt if I have ever seen him bowl so consistently well as in his last home series, against New Zealand in 1983.

His unswerving concentration to the task in hand sometimes led him into unfortunate incidents. When he hit Iqbal Qasim in the face with a bouncer at Edgbaston in 1978, he stayed away from the unfortunate batsman as we examined his bloodied face. Bob said afterwards that the sight of blood on the pitch would have distracted him and reduced his bowling effectiveness. That was wrong, in my opinion. Iqbal Qasim was only an obdurate tail-ender and Bob was far too good a bowler to need recourse to such tactics. Worse still, he ought to have shown some compassion because it looked an ugly injury. Anybody who didn't know Bob Willis would have assumed from that incident that he was an uncaring harsh fellow, but that wasn't so. In my experience, he has been one of the most sporting cricketers of my time, who hardly ever gave the umpire a moment's trouble. When, upon taking over the England captaincy, he wielded the big stick about behaviour, he was only asking the others to do what he had invariably managed to do throughout his career.

Very much an old-fashioned cricketer with entrenched views, Bob was a great man for efficiency over style. For him, it would always be John Edrich ahead of David Gower, Geoff Boycott instead of Graham Gooch and Basil D'Oliveira in preference to Ian Botham. This wasn't meant to denigrate the younger element, it was more the reaction of a fast bowler who didn't like tearing in at people like Edrich, who would block you out for the first hour or so, then capitalise on your fatigue. Bob would always prefer to bowl at the likes of Gower, who gave you some hope early on with one or two streaky shots. Bob's strong views were invariably much the same as mine, especially on things like respect for tradition in the game, the need for sportsmanship and a fairer contest between bat and ball. Inevitably a man of such positive views would have one or two blind spots. He inherited one from Mike Brearley with Phil Edmonds and I can't understand what possessed him to go to Australia in 1982–83 with three off-spinners, or with a military medium-pacer like Robin Jackman who proved to be predictably ineffective on good, hard wickets. He had little time for those who didn't work hard at their cricket, but his hands were a little tied during his reign as England captain. I felt he deserved a far better fate than his sad, early homecoming from Pakistan in the spring of 1984. History will judge him more kindly as a captain and nobody will ever be able to question his record as a fast bowler. I don't think

I ever played with a braver cricketer, one who made less fuss about his injuries. England never had a greater trier in my time.

David Gower

David Gower has been an adornment to the England side ever since he joined us in the Pakistan series of 1978 and pulled his first ball to the boundary. He fitted in straightaway, with that easy, likeable manner of his; Brearley handled him very well and Boycott seemed to take a shine to him. Both these shrewd men obviously recognised supreme natural talent when they saw it. We were fortunate that the Packer Revolution had left a vacuum for David to fill in the England side. In another era, he might have had to wait a long time to get in and his lack of consistent runs at county level might have precluded him from a long run in the England team. The conservative element could have considered him too flashy for the rigours of Test cricket. David has sometimes given that impression. He is still vulnerable in the gully area, where he tends to slice his drives or fails to get over the cut. Both these defects stem from faulty footwork; David relies on his natural gift for timing, rather than the essential orthodoxies of moving the feet into the textbook position. As a result, he can struggle against the seamers on green wickets, and that is why his Test record is more impressive on the quicker wickets abroad.

I didn't agree with saddling David with the captaincy when they took it away from Bob Willis. He did a good salvage operation in Pakistan, when we were ravaged by illness and injury, but I am sure he would agree that the players' own professionalism surfaced at last and made the job a little easier for him. Mike Gatting was also an invaluable help as his number two. David ran into a rich vein of form at that time, which inevitably helped in his dealings with the team. I believe David accepted that the luck ran for him at last and that it had worked out better than he could have imagined. It was wrong to assume that that short-term success in Pakistan equipped him for a home series as captain against West Indies. We needed his batting to be at its very best, but inevitably he was dragged down by the cares of captaining a weak side against an all-powerful one. It is always easier to captain England for the first time on a tour, away from the glare of publicity, yet David was pitched right in at the deep end. Quite apart from that, I'm not sure that David is captaincy material. Although he has a good cricket brain, he is a fairly casual character. On tour, he often used to be late for nets, official functions or team dinners and I think it will be difficult for this particular leopard to change his spots with responsibility thrust upon him. Only time will tell.

Basically he is too good a player to be distracted by the job, no matter how prestigious it might seem to David. Heaven knows, we are short enough of class as it is. I would hate to think that the captaincy would coincide with a continued decline in his batting, because David Gower at his best is one of the great sights of English cricket.

Phil Edmonds

Phil Edmonds has been a fool to himself over the years, even though I believe he has been handled badly. He has been labelled the 'Bad Boy' of English cricket and, although he has deserved some of the stigma, I feel he shouldn't have been denied so many England tours. I can think of one or two players who have still accumulated caps when they were far from being the most popular guys on the circuit. Why Phil Edmonds should lose out is a mystery to me; all he needs is strong handling and a warning of the consequences if he steps out of line. In return, England would have got the best out of a fine allround cricketer – a clean striker of the ball, a brilliant fielder in any position and a class slow left-arm bowler. His tenacity and fighting spirit would also have been invaluable at times: I don't think he would smile defeat away as easily as some of the others.

I must admit I have never been on the same wavelength as Phil, but I never thought I would be. I was twice with him on England tours and once when with the International Wanderers in South Africa, and we were hardly close. In background we were poles apart and I felt that at times he was unnecessarily haughty and sarcastic. He did himself no favours on the 1978–79 tour of Australia under Mike Brearley. In the First Test, he bowled two bouncers without telling me; I stopped one of them and the other went for four byes. Mike went spare at him, but it made no difference. They fell out again at Perth in the next Test. Phil had been made twelfth man and his attitude towards his duties was, to say the least, somewhat cavalier. We came off after one particularly tense session to find Phil with his feet up, having done nothing about drinks. Mike tore a strip off him and I'm sure some of the crowd outside heard the ructions. It was all water off a duck's back to Phil, and that incident finished him on the tour. He practised fairly rigorously, but didn't get another look in as Miller and Emburey bowled so well. Obviously all that got back to Lord's because Edmonds didn't tour again for another six years, and three more England captains after Brearley.

Phil seems to have a professional deathwish. When he got back into the England team in 1982, he should have realised that he was on trial under the captaincy of Bob Willis, a man who had little time for him. That didn't stop Phil giving some verbals to Dilip Vengsarkar in the First Test, at Lord's, against the Indians. Vengsarkar threw down his helmet and stepped away from the wicket after Phil had been trying to gee everyone up; Phil then lobbed in a few unsavoury words. That was wrong, it was games-manship and I can't understand why he felt he had to do it. He got a rocket from Peter May, the new chairman of the selectors, and was dropped after three Tests. The following summer, he forced his way back into the side by bowling brilliantly for Middlesex. He was picked at the Oval to play against New Zealand and proceeded to astonish us with his antics. In the first session of their innings, he started shouting encouragement at no one in particular from mid-wicket; he would shout, 'Come on, watch that one' or 'He's suspect there' or 'He can't play a shot there, you know.' Obviously he was nervous and keyed up, but he was walking around, looking up at the sky shouting at no one in particular. The slips and I kept looking over at him, wondering if he was feeling all right. When he came on to bowl in the first innings, he was smashed around by Richard Hadlee and proceeded to bowl two bouncers in a row without warning. I parried one of them, took the other and Richard Hadlee just grinned. I wasn't amused – it was Brisbane 1978 all over again – and our captain must have wondered why he'd brought him back in the side to act the fool again. It was particularly daft, considering that he was very much on trial and that any naughty stuff would be viewed with grave concern. Many of Phil's detractors were just waiting to write him off, and here he was digging his own grave. When he developed back trouble and Nick Cook succeeded him with such striking success, I thought that was the end of his Test career. On cricketing grounds, I am glad he forced his way back a year later to go on the tour of India.

Phil is still very unfulfilled as a cricketer. He gets easily bored and has the temperament of a fast bowler rather than of a spinner. He might have made a good captain, considering his combative nature and the fact that he doesn't care about popularity contests.

His name always seems to be bandied about for other counties, but I would be surprised if he leaves London. He loves the cultural side of London and the commercial attractions of the capital city. On basic ability, he ought to have about fifty caps. I believe selectors should pick the best men for each tour, irrespective of their temperaments, and then back the captain in any action he takes. If that had been so, then Phil Edmonds would probably have been busy every winter on England tours.

Tony Greig

Tony Greig bears a fair amount of responsibility for the decline in sportsmanship in the English game. He was the first England player I remember actively indulging in gamesmanship. He stood very close in at bat-pad position and would appeal for everything. He was the same as a bowler – the object was to pressurise the umpires into making mistakes. When he batted he would stand there and wait for the decision even though he had knocked the cover off the ball. Very South African, whatever his English qualifications.

I toured three times with Greigy and there was no doubt that he had the knack of leadership. In West Indies in 1973–74 and again in Australia a year later, he had a far more positive effect than the captain, Mike Denness, and I considered it only a matter of time before he got the job. He was flamboyant, charming with the media, a crowd pleaser and worth his place in the team as an allrounder. The England lads who played under him thought Greigy great value and I am afraid that his gamesmanship rubbed off on some of them. When I returned to the England scene after a gap of two and a half years, I noticed how much harder they all played – and that included dubious appeals and the verbals if necessary. I hadn't forgotten how Greigy tricked out Eddie Barlow in a John Player League match a year earlier. Eddie played the ball to backward square-leg and set off for a single. Greig went straight across the pitch and ran into Barlow; Eddie couldn't get past him and he was run out by the throw from square leg. I wrote in my captain's report that the England skipper had been guilty of ungentlemanly conduct, that he had barged into Eddie deliberately. I thought it was a disgraceful action and told him so. Unfortunately, Greigy was no stranger to such tricks and his influence soon spread. If the England captain could stand at silly point, mouthing off at a batsman, why shouldn't the rest follow suit? And what's wrong with pointing to the pavilion after dismissing someone?

Tony Greig's disrespect for the traditions of cricket meant he was right up Kerry Packer's street and the current captain of England was soon hooked on the idea of World Series Cricket. He wouldn't have had the dilemma that Keith Fletcher did in 1982 about the South African offer. Greigy was always one to accommodate the highest bidder and I saw evidence of that early in his career. We toured Australia together with the Rest of the World side, in 1971–72, and one day he sat next to me in the plane and raved about the country. He said he was thinking of packing up the game and moving out to Australia, where there were so many opportunities to make a fortune. He said there was more to life than cricket, even though he had hardly been a professional for five minutes. He said he liked the Australian attitude towards life; you could make a pile of cash without being made to feel sheepish about it. The seeds of his involvement with Packer were sown years before he ever met the man.

Geoff Miller

Geoff Miller has spent a long time trying to consolidate a place in the game that I think he can reach. He was my team-mate at Derbyshire for more than a decade and my partner on several England tours, and I can honestly say that he should have been one of our leading players. Time and again, Geoff would show his class with bat or his off-spin, then fall away, easily discouraged. He bowled beautifully on the 1978–79 tour of Australia, even better than John Emburey, yet he hasn't got anywhere near that standard since. I think he's a fine bowler, yet he can't seem to take punishment; he goes into his shell and bowls flat. As a batsman, he has the natural ability of a genuine middle-order man at Test level, yet we had that nonsense about his maiden hundred. I have batted twice with him when he's got into the nineties with England, and each time he has frozen. In the Derbyshire dressing-room we tried all sorts of ways to get him over that psychological hurdle. Sometimes we wouldn't mention it to him if he was near the hundred, other times we'd tell him that he should just take his time and he would get the remaining handful of runs. It never seemed to work. It was ridiculous that I broke the barrier of my maiden hundred three years before Geoff, a man I have seen play beautifully all over the world.

He almost left us in 1981, when he resigned the Derbyshire captaincy because the pressures got to him. Like me, he found it hard to captain mates he had grown up with over the years, and he lacked the killer instinct. He says he's learned a lot now and that he could tackle the job again. We haven't seen the best of Geoff Miller as allrounder, nor captain. He has the ability to do the double once he sorts out his approach to the game and realises you can't be up one day and down the next.

For all that, Geoff has been a great chap to play cricket with, a sportsman who respected the spirit in which the game should be played. It was fitting that on the day I finished my first-class career he should be the first man to congratulate me as we walked off the field. He shook my hand and said, 'Bob, thanks very much for everything – it's been a privilege to play with you.' I appreciated that gesture more than he would ever realise and it summed up the decency of the man.

Mike Hendrick

Mike Hendrick was, like Geoff Miller, another of my good friends and team-mates who could never stay consistently at the top. Mike had bags of talent, with a lovely bowling action, but the mystery remained: why didn't he do even better? He never seemed to get match-winning figures. He would deserve seven wickets but have to make do with three. I think that stemmed from the fact that he bowled the wrong length and from the wrong angle. He would bowl from wide of the crease and slant the ball in at a spot about nine inches outside the off stump; time after time he would beat the batsmen all ends up with a 'nip-backer' but it would go over the top of the stumps. I have seen Alec Bedser try to sort out his problem on tours. He would place a hankie on a spot and tell Hendo to hit the spot. Hendo used to snigger at Alec's old-fashioned ways but he was wrong to doubt a man who had taken 236 Test wickets. He was always one yard too short and the batsman could either play him off the back foot or miss it by a long way. He never seemed to get them playing half-back, half-forward to a ball that was starting to deviate. Like Australia's Max Walker, Hendo couldn't get them to snick him with any degree of regularity. As a result, he got comparatively few wickets, even though he beat batsmen so many times.

I was sorry to see him leave Derbyshire, but thought the move to the green wickets at Trent Bridge might galvanise him. Unfortunately it didn't really work out and the old injury jinx hit him again. Hendo has never been consistently fit and the stock phrase in our dressing-room used to be, 'If only we had Hendo with us on this wicket.' He never seemed to be there because of injury. One day, Eddie Barlow called a meeting of the First XI and told us about Hendo's injury problems. He told us that he had been advised not to do a lot of net practice because he had to go easy on his hip. Eventually he developed an arthritic hip which dogged the latter part of his career. It was a great shame, because Hendo was a real trier, despite his languid appearance. With a little more luck with injuries and a different bowling length, Mike Hendrick would have been a consistently great bowler.

Dennis Lillee

Dennis Lillee was the last word in consistency throughout a marvellous career as a truly great fast bowler. Our Test careers began and ended more or less at the same time. He made his debut on Ray Illingworth's tour and was still bowling against England in December 1982. He looked a promising performer in 1970 yet when I returned to Australia the following year with the Rest of the World side he had improved tremendously. At Perth he bowled us out for 59, taking eight for 29 against a batting line-up that saw Sobers at number seven and Intikhab at number nine. On the way back to the hotel, my taxi driver started off about Lillee, telling me that we Poms had nobody to match him. I said, 'Look mate, come back to me in ten years' time when he's taken wickets against all countries in all conditions – then we'll see if he's a great bowler.' I never saw that taxi driver again, but my scepticism proved unfounded. Yet I thought he was finished just a month later, when he broke down at Sydney with back trouble. I saw him back at the hotel and he looked a pathetic sight, wearing a corset to support his back. I sympathised with him and he said, 'It looks like the end for me, I'm in real agony.' It just shows the character of the man that he could come back after that and other injuries in later years.

He gave a remarkable demonstration of his prowess in South Africa with the International Wanderers in 1976. Dennis had arrived from the gruelling home series against West Indies that the Aussies had won five-one, and I wondered if Dennis would treat this short tour as a holiday, and just coast along. Not a bit of that; the attitude of all the Australians was magnificent and, at a game in Benoni, Dennis showed he was the complete fast bowler. Glenn Turner was captaining the side and was astonished to be told by Dennis that he didn't want a fine leg or a third man, two positions that are normally occupied for an opening bowler. When Glenn asked why, he was told, 'I shan't bowl down there,' and Dennis was as good as his word. He bowled a beautiful line, on or just outside the off stump and he was far too good for the batsmen.

I've always liked Dennis Lillee off the pitch, yet he's been a real pain in the neck on the field of play at times. He went way over the top in 1974–75 against Mike Denness' side – all that gesticulating and pointing to the pavilion was ridiculous. At Perth in 1979, his nonsense with the aluminium bat was unbelievable. No one could believe it when this cream-coloured bat made a clanging sound when it hit the ball. Even Greg Chappell, his captain, was stunned and he came onto the pitch to make Lillee use a proper bat. It was all part of a gimmick designed to get customers for the aluminium bat, but Lillee made a complete fool of himself by trying to goad Mike Brearley, then flinging the bat away in a mock temper. It was a totally theatrical performance for the benefit of the cameras and Lillee had the cheek to feign a loss of temper. He was up to his tricks again at Edgbaston in 1981, when he rounded on me in a rage after I had told him to stop slagging off Graham Gooch, who had appealed for a catch off Lillee. Clearly he needed to be goaded into some sort of controlled fury so that he could do himself justice as a bowler, but that was all far too deep for me.

After that Edgbaston Test, we saw the other side of Lillee, when he charmed everyone at the benefit dance for Bob Willis. When he wasn't on the field, Dennis Lillee was a very nice man indeed. His ability as a bowler was so massive that he didn't really need the theatricals.

Rodney Marsh

Rodney Marsh was one of my favourite cricketers. A gritty, hard character, he was a lot softer than many realised and was a fairer opponent than many of his Australian colleagues. He was always first through the dressing-room door with a beer in his hand, no matter what had happened on the field of play earlier on, and he would never stint on sincere congratulations.

I was enormously impressed at the way Rod knuckled down

to the job of keeping wicket. When I first saw him in 1970–71 he was unfairly dubbed 'Iron Fists' by people who didn't understand his problems. A massively built man – Alan Knott or I could stand behind him and no one would see us – he had to come to terms with the physical demands of the job. He was given some awful throws from the outfield by a poor fielding side, and many made unfavourable and unfair comparisons with Knotty. When we returned four years later, Marsh was a tremendous keeper. He had slimmed down and his athleticism in taking deliveries that dipped and swerved was most impressive. His hands were black and blue from the continual pounding from Lillee and Thomson, but he was a tough man. The marvellous professionalism of Lillee, his Western Australia teammate, had rubbed off on him and he was now a dedicated cricketer. I am sure that the competition provided by his golfing brother, Graham, spurred him on. I had dinner with the Marsh family on that 1974–75 tour and Rod was astonished to learn about Graham's earning power from just a casual remark. Graham was just off to Japan and he happened to mention how much he would be earning. Rod said that it would take him a couple of series to earn what Graham was about to pick up for three days' golf. So when Kerry Packer came along, he didn't have to look far for his Australian keeper.

A great team man, Rod Marsh. Dennis Lillee has often acknowledged the shrewdness of Rod's observations on the game and he must have picked up a lot of wisdom standing beside Ian Chappell for so many years. Thankfully, he rarely indulged in the kind of ugly histrionics that Chappell and Lillee seemed to think necessary to win a Test. I envied Rod's ability to hit the ball like a shell and considered him one of the most dangerous batsmen at number seven in my Test era. As a keeper, he lacked facility to the spinners, but that is more of a comment on the age in which he has played his cricket. Spring-heeled dives from 20 yards back have become more common than leg-side stumpings, more's the pity. His ratio of victims to Tests has been astonishingly high and I can hardly remember him dropping a catch in the series we played together. He may not have looked too elegant behind the stumps but, my word, he was mighty effective.

Sunil Gavaskar
Sunil Gavaskar was the best opening batsman I saw in my career. He was a combination of Geoffrey Boycott and Barry Richards;

the grace of Richards and the concentration of Boycott. He was so neat, well-organised and stylish. I could watch Gavaskar bat all day, preferably in a game that didn't involve England! For long periods, he carried his country's batting and, unlike Boycott, never gave the impression that it was a super-human task.

You would think that Gavaskar's height would be a disadvantage and it is true that the West Indians and Bob Willis could occasionally tuck him up and trouble him with deliveries aimed at his heart. Yet he was a great leaver of the ball – rocking back and forth to the short-pitched delivery, as if he had all the time in the world. I remember a magnificent duel between Sunil and Bob Willis at Madras in 1982. We desperately needed to break through in the series and at last we had a pitch that favoured the seamers on the first morning. Bob Willis tore in and bowled very quickly at Sunil, but he held out in a masterly display of defensive batting. At lunch, India were 49 for one and, although Sunil soon went afterwards for 25, he had done the difficult job of drawing the teeth of our fast attack. India ended up with 481 for four declared but the outstanding innings was one of just 25.

I have always enjoyed playing cricket against Sunil, even when he occasionally exasperated us in 1982 with his defensive captaincy after taking an early lead in the series. He was too old a hand to let that one slip. A gentle man, with a nice droll sense of humour, he pulled Geoffrey Boycott's leg on that tour about his record total of runs. Sunil knew how much it meant to Boycott to overtake Garry Sobers' record of Test runs and watched him lap up all the adulation. Finally, at a celebration dinner to mark Boycott's achievement, Sunil made a charming speech and said, 'Make the most of it, Geoffrey – you won't have it for very long.' It was said in Sunil's usual disarming manner, but there was no mistaking the message. Two years later, he had not only passed Boycott's runs total but beaten Sir Donald Bradman's record of 29 Test centuries. It would never do to underestimate Sunil Gavaskar.

CHAPTER 13

WICKETKEEPING AND BATTING

Now this is a vexed question: should a wicketkeeper sacrifice the prospect of further improvement by trying to develop his batting? It is a dilemma that has robbed me of England caps: I have suffered because of batting defects in the England set-up. Such a situation accelerated my retirement in 1984. I still felt I was good enough behind the stumps and I cherished the hope that I would get to play at least one Test against West Indies, thereby completing my set of Test countries, but there is no sentiment in top cricket. Paul Downton was selected on batting potential rather than actual achievement – his career average of 18 was just one run more than mine. There was no criticism of my wicketkeeping and it was clear that the selectors thought that Paul could do a better job with the bat against the West Indian fast bowlers. They were proved right; Paul battled hard, occupied the crease for long periods and justified the selectors' faith in him. I do not feel he is the best young keeper around, but I could understand why they went for Paul. He had been on two full England tours, absorbed much of the atmosphere and had experience of batting in Tests against West Indies in 1980–81. When I saw how well he fared as a batsman in the First Test in 1984, I knew I wouldn't get back in again for that series. Paul deserved a long run. Derbyshire knew my feelings on the matter and my retirement was announced, with no ill-feeling. With the greatest respect to my county, I needed the adrenalin from Tests to keep me going at the age of 43 and I was worried that the alternative was a slow slide downhill. I still felt my work as a wicketkeeper was good enough and I was pleased that my last victim in first-class cricket was a stumping. A week later, I took a catch in a benefit game that was one of the best I could ever remember. Geoff Tedstone, Warwickshire's reserve wicketkeeper, glanced a ball and I took off to catch it in my left hand. That was the last game I stood in as a serious keeper and I was happy to go out on a high note.

Should I have slackened off in my training as a keeper and tried to improve my batting? For me, the answer is categorically 'No': I had natural ability as a keeper, whereas my batting was a bonus if it came off. A career batting average of 17 hardly indicates I was in the rabbit category and eventually I worked out my limitations and a way to bat competently. I could never play the hook shot, the short-pitched delivery aimed straight at me would often get me in difficulties and I lacked the power of strokes of a Bairstow. Yet I could play easily enough off my legs, I played the cut productively and I could off-drive when the ball was in the right spot. My good footwork meant I was happier at home against the spinners, as I could get down the wicket to them. I think the damage was done to my batting in my first decade in county cricket. My wicketkeeping was always most important to Derbyshire, because of our tradition of long-serving performers. The career average of George Dawkes worked out at 18, while his predecessor, Harry Elliott, was just short of 14. Their job was to keep wicket for many years and I was no different. Any runs that came my way were treated as a bonus and that is why I was an irresponsible batsman for a long time. I got myself out through a lack of concentration, even though I felt I tried my best all the time. A rush of blood was often my trouble, as the chase for bonus points with overs running out dictated my approach.

After my first tour as England number one in 1978, Mike Brearley told the media that I ought to bat higher up the order for Derbyshire because I would benefit from the extra responsibility. That was easy for him to say, but Derbyshire needed to think about the other batsmen who needed the experience. It would have been unfair to a young allrounder, struggling to prove himself in the first team, if I had gone ahead of him. I realised that Brearley wanted to add some depth to the England batting and that it looked a little vulnerable with me coming in at number seven, but I felt my main responsibility was behind the stumps. I didn't want to run the risk of a deterioration in my standards, just because I was batting further up the order. In all honesty, I don't really think I had it in me to be a better batsman; I lacked that extra something, whether it was Alan Knott's gift of improvisation or the eye of David Bairstow. Test cricket definitely helped me improve my batting, but it was never going to be of match-winning quality. My best innings have been played in a supporting role, where temperament and courage were more vital than glamorous strokes. Due to the weakness of the England batting, I had to get my head down and graft and, whatever the records say, I improved a good deal after 1977. The need to concentrate against Test bowlers brought out my competitive instinct and I was pleased that I gained the reputation of being difficult to dislodge.

I consider myself fortunate to have started in the game when there was less pressure on the keeper to be a good bat as well. There was no limited-overs cricket in 1961, and we didn't have all three one-day competitions until 1972, so I had time to concentrate on my skills. If I was beginning my career in the 1980s, I am sure that the coach or the captain would be getting on to me about my batting. The need to hit the medium-pacers over the top, or to crash a good length ball over mid-wicket would be judged almost as important as a leg-side stumping. The counties are sacrificing specialist keepers on the altar of batting effectiveness, and I might just have struggled to break through today. At the start of my county career, I was just a neat, orthodox tailender; today that wouldn't be good enough, there are hardly any rabbits in the first-class game anymore. I believe the present crop of young wicketkeepers is as good as at any time in my career, but they will need to be strong-minded to avoid a deterioration of skill for the sake of batting. Jack Richards is an example of this trend. When he toured India with England, I was very impressed by his willingness to learn and to concentrate on his gifts. Since then, Jack has realised his batting needed improvement if he was going to get international recognition and his average has steadily climbed. Yet I think his wicketkeeping has gone back a little in the process – he seems to dive rather too much now for my liking. I always have a chat with Jack when I see him and he never fails to ask me for my opinion on his performance that day. Because I like him and respect his professional attitude, I tell him the truth, that he should stay on his feet a little more. He should anticipate, rather than need to dive. I am not the only one to spot Jack's alteration in technique; the first-class umpires are very good judges, and the former keepers among them have confirmed this with me. I am sure that batting has something to do with this: Jack has to spend more time in the nets and his work with the gloves must inevitably suffer. Promotion up the order means he has less time to recover for the physical strains of keeping wicket, and diving for the ball replaces anticipation. When you are tired, you do not anticipate as well; you rely on reactions, rather than thinking about what might happen.

It really is expecting a lot of a keeper to bat anywhere in the first six. I know Les Ames was a marvel for Kent for so many seasons between the wars, but he didn't have to contend with so many different forms of professional cricket, nor the amount of short-pitched fast bowling that wears you down after a time. Jim Parks managed it for a period, but he was a batsman before he became a keeper and no one would ever say that he became a specialist behind the stumps. His main asset was standing back to the seamers, relying on his athleticism. Alan Knott preferred to bat no higher than number seven, and rightly so. I felt sorry for Jock Edwards and Bruce Edgar when they alternated with the gloves on the 1978 New Zealand tour to this country. Neither would claim to be a genuine keeper, but they had to don the gloves as well as get some runs. Jock failed at both, then Bruce had to take over for the final Test, at Lord's. He opened the innings, then stood behind the stumps for a long time as we built up a useful lead. After keeping wicket for more than four hours on the third day, he had to open the innings with just under two hours left that night. He was in no frame of mind for the task and Ian Botham bowled him almost immediately. It was a waste of one of their best batsmen and unfair to expect a wicketkeeper to take on such an onerous task – even if it was true that he had enjoyed a close view of the wicket from behind the stumps. You can't legislate for physical and mental fatigue.

I have always told young keepers that batting must inevitably come second if they are to make their mark in the game. I realise this stems from my conviction that cricket should be a game for specialists, rather than the bits-and-pieces men that seem to be flourishing nowadays. My feeling is that if you are good enough behind the stumps, they can't possibly leave you out. The runs you save by your own example and the inspiration you give to the fielders can be priceless. If you drop a half-chance off Viv Richards before he has scored and you then go out and slog an attractive thirty, it doesn't mean the specialist keeper should be out of favour. The specialist would have more chance of taking the half-chances and turning the game, so that he might make few runs is academic. The best way to win a cricket match is to get the opposition back in the pavilion as soon as possible, and you accomplish that by having a class wicketkeeper backing up class bowlers. No less an authority than *The MCC Cricket Coaching Book* says so: 'It can therefore be laid down as an absolute principle in team selection that the best wicketkeeper, irrespective of all other considerations, should always be chosen.' Would that it were so. Yet in my capacity as holder of the Advanced Coaching Certificate, I do not deviate from that principle. Batting is, of course, important and I would encourage every player to try to improve in that direction. Yet class wicket-keepers are born, not made and they have to be appreciated. It is a denial of one of the game's great skills to give preference to an athlete who can bat, but is slipshod when he stands up to the stumps and tries to make sense of a spinner or an off-cutter.

On a county staff, the young keeper relies on the senior one for advice and help in practice. In a sense we are a breed apart – the bowlers and batsmen just glance at us practising and let us get on with it. My successor, Bernie Maher, knows my views on batting and keeping wicket. I have told him that I fully expect him to still be keeping for Derbyshire by the year 2000 – taking the county through 80 years with just four keepers. That will be a record any county would be proud of, and I have told Bernie that he can do it, provided he remembers that Messrs Elliott, Dawkes and Taylor did their best with the bat but were first and foremost wicketkeepers.

I would love to see Bernie follow me into the England team one day, but we will just have to wait and see how he shapes up to the daily rigours of first-class cricket over a few seasons. If I had to pick out one keeper from a talented bunch, I would go for Jack Russell of Gloucestershire. He always impresses me when I see him. He has the ideal build, is neat and unobtrusive, with the ability to stay on his feet most of the time. He gets a fair amount of experience standing up to the spinners in Gloucester-shire – 17 stumpings in his first full season – and he has no qualms about standing up to some seamers as well. He doesn't play for a fashionable county, but neither did I, and the selectors still noticed me. He has a very good pair of hands and always seeks out Alan Knott and myself for advice and a general chat. He is one lad who thinks he can learn from the old 'uns, but then we wicketkeepers have always had a special bond between us! Jack's batting has improved and I hope he soon gets an England tour to give him greater experience. I honestly believe that the stan-dard of wicketkeeping in this country is high. Some critics say that they don't get too much chance to stand up nowadays, but I think you'll find that our recent fine summers have meant more spin bowling at county level. Regrettably the trend isn't followed in the Tests, where fast bowling seems to reign supreme. There is a group of very good young keepers around at the moment – David East, Bruce French, Paul Downton, Bobby Parks, Jack Richards and Jack Russell to name but six. They can all bat, but they have the natural ability to become high-class specialists. They need to remember that extra practice is necessary, but it doesn't have to be in the batting nets. How often do we see an opening batsman turn in long, hard practice stints with the ball? Do the fast bowlers knuckle down to the task and really concentrate at batting after a hard session at their specialist job? Of course not; there are allrounders to do that sort of donkey work. Yet the keeper is expected to be master of one trade and more than useful at the other. Only Ian Botham has managed to open the bowling and score centuries for England in the same matches during my career – so why should wicketkeepers be under the kind of batting pressure that fast bowlers never experience? Let cricket be the game for specialists. There is more to keeping wicket than batting at number six and standing alongside slip, wearing a pair of pads. If you don't believe me, look in the MCC coaching book.

CHAPTER 14

THE GENERATION GAP

For the first time in more than 30 years, I have to face up to a life without wicketkeeping. I have played my last serious match as a keeper and only the occasional benefit or charity match will tempt me back behind the stumps. It was a matter of pride that I should go out of the game before any hints were dropped to me. I will still be actively involved in the county scene, as Derbyshire's second team captain – but I shall bat at number eleven and stay away from the wicketkeeper's gloves. That will give a younger man a chance and me the opportunity to try to solve one of English cricket's biggest problems: the attitude of the young players.

Now I know that, in some quarters, I shall be accused of living in the past, but I think that would be unfair. I am certain that England won't improve in world terms until the younger players rediscover professional pride. There is no shortage of talent, but too many now seem to think that the game owes them a living and that they're doing us all a favour by turning out. Over the last few years, I have seen this slapdash attitude grow at county and Test level. It was particularly noticeable on my last two England tours, where defeat was shrugged off and no effort made to learn any lessons. Mine is not the only voice to utter such complaints: Bob Willis has often spoken out about the younger generation and my conversations on the county circuit with the old hands confirm this trend. Managers, coaches and senior pros all agree with me: in our time, there has never been a worse period for bad behaviour and gamesmanship on the field, sloppy practice and obsession with money. Too many of the younger generation want to pick up the rich pickings without doing the hard graft that qualifies them for such rewards.

I shall be doing my best to reverse the trend at Derbyshire. This is still a gentleman's game, to be played as hard as possible by nice people who can also be good sportsmen, ambassadors for their profession. To that end, I have prepared a paper for all the young players at Derbyshire which sets out what is expected of them. I have covered all the aspects of a young pro's responsibilities – his attitude to net practice, the standard of dress that is acceptable at various functions, the proper diet, the duties of a twelfth man, and how he should behave towards members of the public. In other words, the kind of things that were drummed into me by the parents of my generation and what I learned when I joined the Derbyshire staff. I don't want to get back to the kind of situation where my first coach, Denis Smith, told me to put my jacket on with the sun beating down, but they are going to have to smarten up their lifestyles and attitudes to their chosen profession. Some of them think it's a laugh when I go on about the wisdom of being in digs close to the county ground, as I was in the early 1960s. They prefer to live a few miles away, eat junk food and keep long hours. They think that such freedom is vital to do yourself justice on the cricket pitch. They don't understand the need to keep fit for fielding, as well as for batting; anyone can stand and smash the ball around for a couple of hours, but then they have to go out and field in tight situations, where every run is vital. I see them struggling at pre-season practice and know the kind of winters they have spent. They express amazement that I can still beat kids half my age at sprinting and cross-country running; to me it is simply a case of getting fit enough to deserve your money. It's the same in any other walk of life.

I shall try very hard not to be a bore about the old days, but they will have to realise that certain values are unchanging over the years. It is very important to win the confidence of the players, to be constructive with them and to wield the big stick only when necessary, though they still have to get things spelt out clearly to them. I don't think it's all their fault, I believe that it's a social problem as well; the Welfare State cushions them over here, so that they don't want to work hard. The fact that Bob Willis and Ted Dexter need the backing of a brewery to try to find a fast bowler is surely indicative. We all know that fast bowlers win Tests nowadays but we can't find any to replace Bob Willis because it's very demanding work. I have seen people like Bob and Dennis Lillee in great pain or near to exhaustion, yet they still battled on to take wickets. It takes a special kind of person to have guts and natural talent in equal measures and not enough youngsters are willing to go through those barriers. I have talked to Andy Roberts and Viv Richards about the way West Indies simply churn out fast bowlers and they tell me it's because they can see a social passport through their efforts. There is so much poverty out in the Caribbean that the ability to bowl the ball at great speed can take them away from all that, and give them a more comfortable life. So they work hard to achieve that goal: what could be more logical or admirable? Viv tells me that whenever he's home in Antigua, a different lad comes into the nets every day and tries to knock his head off; they want to be noticed, to achieve something by putting one over on the great man. Over here, there's no incentive in their eyes – they leave school, try looking for a job and, when they fail, sign on the dole, ending up in a rut of boredom. They opt for the easy life of watching the television all day, lolling around. To me the prestige, the money and the opportunities for travel are so irresistible today that I can't understand why so few are attracted to the idea of working hard to become an international cricketer. On the rare occasions when a county unearths a genuine fast bowling prospect, he seems to be coached out of his natural talent. Andy Roberts feels that our coaches should just allow a youngster to run in and get the ball to the other end as fast as possible. After that, you can worry about line and length. Andy feels that over here we worry too much about keeping down the runs and forget that fast bowlers can simply blast through a side. He thinks that, until we sort out our coaching and find some youngsters with a real commitment, we shall struggle in this department.

I do get annoyed when I hear a lad on a county staff say, 'Yes, but it's a different game nowadays.' That seems to be enough for him, that's the stock reaction to any words of constructive criticism. Of course it's a different game, but the likes of Dennis Amiss, Keith Fletcher, Jack Simmons, Alan Ormrod and myself could play for more than two decades and still hold our places. Good players can adapt to any era; I'd like to see how one of the young cynics would tackle the problems that Basil D'Oliveira experienced when he first came over from South Africa before knuckling down to becoming an England player within six years. They don't seem to realise that the principles of cricket are basically the same, whatever the era. You have to work very hard at your technique in practice, you must keep yourself fit at all times to play the game, and you must watch those who have

158

proved themselves at the highest level. Boycott and Amiss still practice as hard as ever; that should be enough for any young lad who has slogged a quick fifty in a John Player League game and thinks he has arrived. That is why I hope my paper will help the young pros, make them get used to the experience of playing cricket for a living. Nothing comes easy, but the rewards today are marvellous if you can get ahead of the pack.

I worry about the attitude of the young pro to the game and to life in general. They don't seem to respect the older players, they feel they know it all. They hardly ever seem to talk cricket, to exchange ideas with lads from other counties. It's logical to me that faults in technique can be discussed with the opposition over a pint afterwards and then worked on in the nets the following day, yet they don't appear to be interested. This has been confirmed to me by friends of my age group from the other counties and by the umpires, who are very friendly chaps and can always be relied on to give a few tips when asked. There is a blasé kind of feeling among the younger element in county cricket. I suppose it stems partly from better education than in my day, which in turn gives them more confidence to go their own way. Travel is partly responsible; these days, their passport is regularly stamped through cricket tours abroad or winter coaching. They come to expect it as a right, without realising how fortunate they are to get paid for an enjoyable, open-air job. I don't believe they appreciate what sponsors do for the game in this country. Time and again, I hear them moaning in the dressing-room when told they have to go up to a sponsor's box at close of play to have a general chat for a few minutes. They fail to understand that sponsorship keeps many cricketers in a job, and that it's human nature that the sponsors would like to talk to players that they have watched from a distance all day. It costs nothing to be pleasant to people who love cricket and are happy to help us out – yet many young players go on about 'earbashing'. If they put themselves out for more people, they might get winter work from the much-maligned local sponsors, but too many of them prefer to slump in the corner and talk among themselves about the latest rock music. It's the same with the England team. Too many of them have come straight into the land of milk and honey, where you get £1,500 a Test. They don't remember the days when you would be out of pocket from a winter tour with England, and fail to understand just how much Cornhill Insurance has done for the top players. Yet a simple request to go into the Cornhill hospitality tent after play has ended invariably starts off the moans about 'earbashing'. The same applies on tour when we have a responsibility to be pleasant to firms and individuals who have made our lives a little easier.

The attitude of some current England players towards practice also leaves something to be desired – and I'm afraid that their example is being copied now at county level. On my last couple of England tours, I was very disturbed at the slipshod work in the nets. Ian Botham would bowl off-breaks, then try to smash every ball out of sight, while David Gower would only bat for a short period, until he knew that his timing was all right. Ian Botham is such a powerful character that the younger, more impressionable members of the side would take their lead from him. As a result, we didn't practice hard enough. I blew my top about this in Pakistan and I like to think that it brought a short-term improvement. From what I could tell, it wasn't maintained under David Gower's captaincy against the West Indians. The hard work put in by Clive Lloyd and his team was a salutary contrast: the best team in the world never slackened off in their training and net practice, while we seemed to think it was a chore. Too many of our best players believe they're doing cricket a favour, they do just enough in the nets to get a sweat on. I was made to feel that we were into overtime if they were asked to do any more. As a result, the standards they set themselves are inevitably lower. The apathy that comes from just turning over your bowling arm is very difficult to lose when the serious stuff starts. I find such an attitude incomprehensible, considering the money and prestige that is now available for playing for your country. In my last few years with England, I was less depressed at actual defeats than with the lack of preparation before and reaction to those defeats. Ian Botham seemed to sum up the cavalier philosophy, which not only harmed his performance but affected less talented team-mates. There must always be room in a side for a genius like Ian Botham, but not at the cost of diluting the team's professionalism.

I noticed one or two other disturbing things on my last tour of Australia. We went to an indoor school in Sydney, run by the former England allrounder Barry Knight, and we watched some great sporting events on film. Barry showed us film of that great Test in 1960 which ended in a tie between Australia and West Indies. There was one revealing moment on that last, tense day when the game could have gone either way. The last over was

bowled by the great Wes Hall, with six runs needed for victory
and three wickets to fall. Richie Benaud, who had batted mag-
nificently, was caught behind and, as he walked past Wes Hall,
he smiled and clearly said, 'Well bowled, Wes' to him. I thought
that was a terrific gesture of sportsmanship in the heat of an epic
battle but some of the England players laughed out loud, they
thought it was corny. They seemed to think that a lack of
sportsmanship made today's players superior, that you don't go
around congratulating the opposition. Well all I could say was
that Wes Hall and Richie Benaud would have improved the
quality of that 1982–83 England team, whether or not they were
deemed dubious because they congratulated opponents. I had
the great pleasure of playing against both men and they proved
that you don't have to be ruthless to be a great player. Those
sneers and titters worried me because it stemmed from a lack of
respect for the way the game should be played. I was less than
impressed with some of their behaviour at various airports on
that tour, when I found myself humping around their cricket
cases while they sat back, barely lifting a finger. It seemed a
general feeling that someone would come along and do the
donkey work for them; they were England cricketers, after all,
and surely weren't expected to carry their own gear? Fortunately
Eddie Hemmings – on his first England tour, but a good old-
fashioned professional – helped me out, along with Bernard
Thomas and Norman Gifford, but we were a fairly unhappy
quartet. It seemed that many of the England players had become
distanced from reality through the money they were earning and
the kid-glove way they were being treated. There was a distinct
lack of discipline.

In the last few years, I have become niggled at the gradual
erosion of the standards that I always found admirable in cricket.
The etiquette of the game seems to be deteriorating: fielders
don't wait for the batsmen to lead them off the field at an
interval, and they don't seem all that willing to give the batsmen
a clap as they walk off. Bowlers stand there, seething and staring
if a batsman hits the ball into his pads, thereby avoiding an lbw
appeal, and they get in the way of the batsman as he runs down
the pitch. It looks ridiculous to see a bowler stand there, with
his hands on his hips, if he's been hit to the boundary. Whether
or not they think they've been unlucky, they should walk
smartly back to their mark and get on with the game. A bowler
who has gone for a few runs should be thinking about his next

delivery rather than indulging in the kind of theatricals we see on the football field. I don't know why they think this psychological pressure – staring at the batsman and trying to look menacing – is likely to bring wickets. The good players have the ability to concentrate and they simply ignore a bowler who gives out the verbals and the black looks. It only serves to make the game look less graceful than it should be.

At Derbyshire, I shall crack down on the young players who launch frivolous appeals at the umpire and then react with dumb insolence to the decision. I shan't condone any verbals, nor a batsman who stands his ground after being given out. I found it dreadful to watch Derek Randall dragging himself away from the crease while looking back at the umpire on his way to the pavilion. I know Derek used to get keyed up and was a bundle of nerves when batting, but there is no excuse for undermining an umpire's authority. When England cricketers get away with that, young pros think they can do the same. At Derbyshire, there will be none of that. I believe there's still room to be a winner and play within the code of conduct that is essential to cricket. I will be very disappointed if any players have to be suspended by Derbyshire through bad behaviour, an event that's almost becoming an epidemic in the English county scene, more's the pity. It's time that young professionals at all the counties learned to play the game in the right spirit. The outstanding cricketers should have no need to indulge in petty niggles, while the mundane player who uses them to cover up his own inadequacies shouldn't be in the game at all. I would like to see renewed respect for the great players of the past, a realisation that flickering film shown during a Test match isn't the true guide to a cricketer's talents. I've sat in the England dressing-room, listening to some players chortling at the action from yesteryear, convincing themselves that the old 'uns couldn't hold a candle to their modern counterparts. That's rubbish. Apart from general athleticism and the obsession with fast, short-pitched intimidatory bowling, the game hasn't changed that radically. It would do some of the younger breed no harm at all to listen now and again to the advice of some of the game's great cricketers of the past. In such a complex game, provided your attitude is right, you can't get enough help.

There is much more to professional cricket than a sponsored car, the generosity of Cornhill Insurance and a good living for five months' work in an English summer. Until this generation rediscovers respect for traditions, a positive attitude towards practice and a burning desire to make the very best of all available talent, then English cricket will continue to struggle in the world rankings. It's people like me, who have had a marvellous life out of the game, who will try to arrest the slump.

STATISTICAL APPENDIX

R. W. Taylor in first-class cricket
1960 to 1984

Compiled by Simon Wilde

	Matches	Inns	Not Outs	Runs	Highest Score	100s	50s	Average	C	St
1960	1	2	0	11	11	—	—	5.50	—	—
1961	17	24	6	205	48	—	—	11.39	47	6
1962	29	36	8	300	44	—	—	10.71	77	3
1963	32	49	6	411	54	—	1	9.56	81	2
1964	23	33	11	359	57	—	1	16.32	58	6
1965	30	48	8	558	48	—	—	13.95	79	7
1966	31	47	5	719	42	—	—	17.12	61	3
1967	23	30	6	442	42	—	—	18.42	63	5
1968	29	35	9	400	52	—	1	15.38	58	8
1969	25	32	8	490	65	—	1	20.42	55	7
1969–70 (Ceylon)	1	2	1	26	19	—	—	26.00	—	1
1970	26	35	5	546	56	—	2	18.20	51	11
1970–71 (Australia/New Zealand)	5	6	0	98	31	—	—	16.33	14	5
1971	24	35	10	619	74	—	3	24.76	48	10
1971–72 (Australia)	7	11	3	128	51	—	1	16.00	21	3
1972	22	35	10	402	58	—	1	16.08	39	11
1973	25	40	6	724	61	—	2	21.29	47	10
1973–74 (West Indies)	3	3	0	69	65	—	1	23.00	5	1
1974	22	33	4	488	54	—	1	16.83	52	3
1974–75 (Australia/New Zealand)	6	5	2	89	27	—	—	29.67	11	1
1975	24	38	5	701	69	—	1	21.24	63	14
1975–76 (South Africa)	4	7	0	196	97	—	1	28.00	18	—
1976	21	36	4	641	72	—	1	20.03	47	10
1977	22	23	4	269	36	—	—	14.16	49	2

1977–78 (Pakistan/New Zealand)	11	13	2	236	45	—	—	21.45	20	1
1978	16	17	1	179	32	—	—	11.19	44	3
1978–79 (Australia)	10	15	2	230	97	—	1	17.69	35	6
1979	14	14	3	286	64	—	1	26.00	31	3
1979–80 (Australia/India)	8	11	1	227	47	—	—	22.70	29	1
1980	21	23	6	241	75	—	1	14.18	35	7
1981	19	22	4	259	100	1	—	14.39	46	12
1981–82 (India/Sri Lanka)	11	10	2	132	40	—	—	16.50	27	1
1982	19	29	5	286	54	—	1	11.92	48	4
1982–83 (Australia)	7	14	5	188	37	—	—	20.89	16	1
1983	21	30	7	366	41	—	—	15.91	49	2
1983–84 (New Zealand/Pakistan)	10	13	1	216	86	—	1	18.00	20	—
1984	18	22	7	303	46	—	—	20.20	28	4
TOTALS	637	878	167	12,040	100	1	23	16.93	1,472	174

Bowling: 1 for 75

The 1971–72 tour was with a Rest of the World side and the 1975–76 tour with the International Wanderers; all others were with either MCC or England sides.

Highest score: 100 Derbyshire v Yorkshire, Sheffield, 1981

Season	Opponents	Venue	Batting		Wicketkeeping (C/St)	
			1st Inns	2nd Inns	1st Inns	2nd Inns
1970–71	v NEW ZEALAND	Christchurch	4	—	2/1	0
1977–78	v PAKISTAN	Lahore	32	—	1/1	1
		Hyderabad	0	—	1	1
		Karachi	36	18*	1	—
1977–78	v NEW ZEALAND	Wellington	8	0	4	0
		Christchurch	45	—	1	1
		Auckland	16	—	1	2
1978	v PAKISTAN	Edgbaston	—	—	3	0
		Lord's	10	—	1	3
		Headingley	2	—	1	—
1978	v NEW ZEALAND	Oval	8	—	1	1
		Trent Bridge	22	—	5	1
		Lord's	1	—	1/1	3
1978–79	v AUSTRALIA	Brisbane	20	—	5	0
		Perth	12	2	3	3
		Melbourne	1	5	1	1/1
		Sydney	10	21*	0	0
		Adelaide	4	97	2	0
		Sydney	36*	—	1/1	2
1979	v INDIA	Edgbaston	—	—	0	1
		Lord's	64	—	3	0
		Headingley	1	—	1	—

Season	Opponent	Venue				
1979–80	v AUSTRALIA	Perth	14	15	3	3/1
		Sydney	10	8	3	1
		Melbourne	23	32	0	0
1979–80	v INDIA	Bombay	43	—	7	3
1981	v AUSTRALIA	Lord's	0	9	3	1
		Headingley	5	1	3	4
		Edgbaston	0	8	1	1
1981–82	v INDIA	Bombay	9*	1	4	3
		Bangalore	33	—	2	—
		Delhi	0	—	1/1	0
		Calcutta	6	—	2	0
		Madras	8	—	2	—
		Kanpur	0	—	1	—
1981–82	v SRI LANKA	Colombo	31*	—	1	2
1982	v INDIA	Lord's	31	1	1	2
		Old Trafford	1*	—	2	2
		Oval	3	—	1	3
1982	v PAKISTAN	Edgbaston	1	54	2	3
		Lord's	5	24*	2	0
		Headingley	18	6*	2	3
1982–83	v AUSTRALIA	Perth	29*	31	1	1
		Brisbane	1	3	3	0
		Adelaide	2	3*	3	1
		Melbourne	1	37	1	0
		Sydney	0	28*	1	1

Season	Opponents	Venue	Batting 1st Inns	Batting 2nd Inns	Wicketkeeping (C/St) 1st Inns	Wicketkeeping (C/St) 2nd Inns
1983	v NEW ZEALAND	Oval	0	—	1	4
		Headingley	10*	9	0	0
		Lord's	16	7	0	2
		Trent Bridge	21	0	0	4
1983–84	v NEW ZEALAND	Wellington	14	—	3	2
		Christchurch	2	15	4	—
		Auckland	23	—	0	0
1983–84	v PAKISTAN	Karachi	4	19	1	0
		Faisalabad	0	—	0	1
		Lahore	1	5	1	0

	Matches	Inns	NO	Runs	HS	100s	50s	Average	C	St
TOTALS	57	83	12	1,156	97	—	3	16.28	167	7

Bowling: 0 for 6

170

Taylor's total of 1,646 dismissals in first-class cricket is a world record. He passed the previous holder of the record, J. T. Murray (who made 1,527 dismissals), on 24 October 1982, when he stumped W. R. Broad, of Queensland, off G. Miller for An England XI at Brisbane.

Taylor's 1,472 catches is also a first-class record. He again took the record from J. T. Murray (1,270 catches), on 21 July 1981, when he caught G. F. Lawson off R. G. D. Willis for England v Australia at Headingley.

Six or more dismissals in an innings:

7 caught   Derbyshire v Glamorgan, Derby, 1966   ⎫ (Derbyshire
           Derbyshire v Yorkshire, Chesterfield, 1975 ⎬ record)
           England v India, Bombay, 1979–80
           (equals world Test record)
6 caught   Derbyshire v Sussex, Chesterfield, 1963
           Derbyshire v Yorkshire, Sheffield, 1983

No other wicketkeeper has made seven or more dismissals in an innings more than once.

Nine or more dismissals in a match:

10 caught Derbyshire v Hampshire, Chesterfield, 1963
           (equals Derbyshire record)
           England v India, Bombay, 1979–80
           (world Test record)
9 caught   Derbyshire v Yorkshire, Chesterfield, 1975

Taylor's total of 174 Test dismissals, in 57 matches, has been bettered for England by only A. P. E. Knott (269 in 95 matches) and T. G. Evans (219 in 91 matches).

The 174 Test dismissals were made with the assistance of the following England bowlers:
60 – I. T. Botham; 38 – R. G. D. Willis; 9 – C. M. Old; 7 – P. H. Edmonds, D. L. Underwood (4c, 3st); 6 – G. R. Dilley, J. K. Lever, G. Miller; 5 – J. E. Emburey (2c, 3st), M. Hendrick, D. R. Pringle; 3 – N. A. Foster; 2 – N. G. B. Cook, N. G. Cowans, R. D. Jackman, K. Shuttleworth, G. B. Stevenson; 1 – G. A. Cope (1st), G. A. Gooch, I. A. Greig, E. E. Hemmings, V. J. Marks, C. L. Smith, P. Willey.

Taylor is the fourth England wicketkeeper, after T. G. Evans, J. M. Parks and A. P. E. Knott, to perform the double of 1000 runs and 100 dismissals in Tests.

Taylor shared in the following century stands in Tests:
171   6th wkt   with I. T. Botham v India, Bombay, 1979–80
                 (record for England–India Tests)

160 6th wkt   with I. T. Botham v New Zealand, Christchurch
                1977–78
135 7th wkt   with G. Miller v Australia, Adelaide, 1978–79
103 8th wkt   with G. Miller v India, Lord's, 1979
Also note:
79   10th wkt with R. G. D. Willis v Pakistan, Edgbaston, 1982
                (record for England–Pakistan Tests)

Taylor took his only first-class wicket as a bowler for Derbyshire v
Gloucestershire at Gloucester in 1984. The batsman, who was caught
by B. Roberts, was A. W. Stovold.